SHORTENED
SEASONS

SHORTENED SEASONS

THE UNTIMELY DEATHS OF MAJOR LEAGUE BASEBALL'S STARS AND JOURNEYMEN

FRAN ZIMNIUCH

TAYLOR TRADE PUBLISHING
Lanham • New York • Boulder • Toronto • Plymouth, UK

Published by Taylor Trade Publishing
An imprint of The Rowman & Littlefield Publishing Group, Inc.
4501 Forbes Boulevard, Suite 200, Lanham, Maryland 20706

Estover Road, Plymouth PL6 7PY, United Kingdom

Distributed by NATIONAL BOOK NETWORK

Library of Congress Cataloging-in-Publication Data

Zimniuch, Fran.
    Shortened seasons : the untimely deaths of major league baseball's stars
and journeymen / Fran Zimniuch.
        p. cm.
    ISBN-13: 978-1-58979-363-7 (pbk. : alk. paper)
    ISBN-10: 1-58979-363-3 (pbk. : alk. paper)
    1. Baseball players—United States—Biography. I. Title.
GV865.A1Z55 2007
796.357092—dc22
[B]   2006029111

∞™ The paper used in this publication meets the minimum requirements of
American National Standard for Information Sciences—Permanence of
Paper for Printed Library Materials, ANSI/NISO Z39.48-1992.

Manufactured in the United States of America.

This is for the loved ones and friends left behind by the players chronicled in these pages.

It is also for those people in my life who had shortened seasons: my father, Eddie, and good friends Bill Wilson, Jim Gallagher, Jack Flanagan, and Carol Neall, who all died long before their time and all of whom I miss.

This is also for those who add joy and happiness to my life, my sons Brent and Kyle.

CONTENTS

CONTENTS

CONTENTS

FOREWORD

In December 1974, I was visiting my family in Los Angeles during the Christmas holiday when I received a phone call from the Houston Astros. I was told that my teammate Don Wilson had died of asphyxiation in his garage, having fallen asleep in the car with the engine running. It appeared to be a suicide, but I didn't believe he would do that. Later, I spoke with another teammate, Jim Ray, who had seen him the previous day. "Don was really fired up," Ray said. "He told me he was in great shape and was planning on having a big year." All I could think was: Why did this happen? Indeed, how did it happen?

I returned to Houston and was a pallbearer at Don's funeral. It was so strange. He didn't even look like the same guy. I guess the cause of death changed his appearance. It changed my world view as well. Suddenly, I realized that I was vulnerable. Whatever symbolic immortality I would achieve on the diamond was dust. One day it would just drift away.

In June 2002, I got another disturbing phone call. Darryl Kile had died of a heart attack in a hotel room in Chicago. This didn't hit quite so close to home, but it still hurt. I had managed Darryl in 1997. He was perhaps the kindest, gentlest player I have ever known. Gone—just like that.

Many of his former teammates flew to St. Louis from all around the country to attend his memorial service. I saw sorrow on their faces. I thought about Darryl's wife, Flynn, and his children. What would they do now?

I was 55 years old at the time and had already had heart surgery and brain surgery. I had come to an understanding of the inevitable. It was different when Don died. I hadn't even considered my own mortality at that time. Now, Darryl's teammates would, perhaps for the first time, realize that they would eventually join him in the ranks of fallen warriors.

In Fran Zimniuch's book, *Shortened Seasons*, there is more than a measure of sweet sorrow. Sweet because the loss of someone you love offers the chance to tap into the deep feelings you had for them, feelings you may not have known were hidden in the folds of your heart and soul.

One of the blessings of the human experience is that we dwell not only in the present, but also in the past and future. The ability to remember and to look forward is one of the things that separates us from the animal kingdom. In this sense, losing a friend puts baseball in its proper place. It is a great game. Some say baseball is life. But until you share the tender moments of grief that come with the deaths of your own family and friends, you may not really realize that relationships are more important than ballgames.

Zimniuch's most recent book, *Richie Ashburn Remembered*, grew from a seed Ashburn left by his grave. What grew was beautiful, and that same beauty lies between the covers of *Shortened Seasons*. For Ashburn, like Wilson and Kile, was a unique and fascinating man. What Zimniuch captures is his life, not his death. In that way, his new book revives the images of baseball heroes who died too soon.

I hope that for you, as with me, this book will not be a funeral, but a celebration of life.

LARRY DIERKER

Preface and
Acknowledgments

Shortened seasons? How did such an idea come into being?

While researching a previous book about baseball great Richie Ashburn, I had the opportunity to learn a great deal about one of my heroes in life. Those who saw him play, listened to his broadcasts, read his newspaper articles, or simply met him on the street felt as if they had a personal relationship with Ashburn. They did not. But from researching his career and speaking with his family, former teammates, and opponents, a private side of a very public man became evident.

When someone we care about dies, the immediate mourning is intense, but then the sorrow fades as we push it into a more comfortable place in our psyche, a place all its own where the loss doesn't hurt quite as much with the passage of time. When you talk to old baseball players about events in their lives, or people who were important, there is almost a panic on their part to ensure that their thoughts are part of some public record. As anyone in any walk of life ages, leaving something behind becomes a goal worth living for.

Any baseball player who achieves a spot on a major league roster, even if just for a single game, is a talented athlete who ranks in the top percentile of his sport. Regardless of what success they achieved in their careers, players should be remembered and their accomplishments appreciated long after those spikes have been hung up.

But life's grim reaper takes no notice of much of anything. When your time is up, your ticket is punched. When an athlete dies, the shock is deeply felt by fans of his sport. But the truism, "Life goes on," continues and before you know it, a fallen player can be forgotten like a fly ball that blows foul in a strong wind. The ump just replaces the baseball and the game goes on. The organization replaces the player and the season goes on.

When a player dies, teammates and fans mourn. But the roster spot is filled and the game goes on for the living. It's a different story for his family and loved ones. *Shortened Seasons* hopes to stop the game long enough to remember some of the people who played it, even if they were unable to play as long as they should have been able to do so. It is meant to remember these players, some of whom have been dead for a century.

Such an undertaking is not an easy task. Research can be an incredibly interesting, albeit a daunting, task. Have I missed some players who fit into the parameters of this undertaking? Hopefully not, but most probably. There are some former baseball players who fought valiantly in the defense of their country. Just some of the names that come to mind include Jimmy Trimble, Eddie Brant, Bun Troy, and Bob Neighbors. But the playing careers of these war heroes either were over or had never begun, as in the case of Trimble.

Two young prospects in the San Diego Padres organization, Gerik Baxter and Mark Hilde, were killed in a horrible automobile accident. But they were each at least a couple of years away from The Show. They certainly deserve to be remembered, but their major league time was not meant to be.

So with the best of intentions, I decided the parameters within which I was working and went off to a maze of research that will forever make me a baseball trivia expert. My friend and mentor Lou

Chimenti, an award-winning journalist, offered great help and his years of journalistic experience to the project.

As is always the case, the folks at the Philadelphia Athletics Historical Society were just a phone call or an e-mail away, offering information on players from years gone by. Ernie Montella and Max Silberman were patient and helpful friends who were as interested in having these players remembered as I was.

The Society for American Baseball Research, better known as SABR, is a wonderful resource for all things baseball. Helpful people like Joe Dittmar and its remarkable Web site opened up a historical gateway for my research.

So many media relations people at major league clubs all across the country were as helpful as they could be in assisting me gather information about many of the players, as well as arranging interviews with former teammates of some of the players who died so young.

And there are so many wonderful publications and Internet venues to gather information that many a night and weekend was spent enjoying eye-opening revelations about times long ago. Some of the many books I've accumulated over the years that offered varying degrees of information include *Total Baseball: The Ultimate Encyclopedia of Baseball*, by John Thorn and Pete Palmer. I have a collection of "Who's Who in Baseball" from every year since 1963. It is one of the few consistent sources for minor league statistics. Bill Lee wrote a fascinating book titled *The Baseball Necrology*, which takes the reader on a sad but interesting journey, teaching readers about the deaths of more than 7,600 baseball players.

The stories of some of the players included on these pages will include many statistics, personal antidotes, and perspectives of the player from teammates, friends, or even relatives. But other players who only had a brief moment in the major league sun many years ago may not have much written about them. Quite frankly, there was very little information available about a number of the players included and literally no teammates left alive to question. But in respect to them, their career, and most important, their lives, I believed it only right to include what little information I was able to learn from some of the various sources already mentioned.

I honestly hope that no one was missed. But much like everyone else, I'm human too and could have overlooked players who belong here. To their memory and families, I apologize, because one of the best parts of this project was having the opportunity to speak with wives, sons, daughters, brothers, and other family members these ballplayers left behind.

Of all the people I want to thank for this project, at the very top of the list are the relatives of the players listed. They were all wonderful to work with. They all appreciated my desire to remember their loved ones and went out of their way to accommodate me, my personal questions, and some painful memories. The pride they had in their lost loved ones shines bright, no matter how many years have passed. Even children of players who never met their fathers, or who are too young to remember them, were filled with pride over the player's career and how his memory lives on in so many people.

Of all the people I had the pleasure to get to know, Donald Bond made perhaps the biggest impression on me. The son of Walt Bond, the powerful first baseman who played with Cleveland, Houston, and Minnesota during a career that was hindered and shortened by leukemia, Donald Bond is now an accountant living and working in the Houston area. He knew his dad and has very fond memories of their time together. But Donald is incredibly proud of both his father the baseball player and his father the person. It is the person Walt Bond was that still causes people to tell his son how nice his dad was to them, or about a special charity function he attended.

To me, the biggest tragedy when death touches a family is the future that is lost. After talking with Donald, I remember thinking, as a father myself, if Walt Bond were alive today, just how much pride he would have in his son and the man he has grown into.

Donald Bond also illustrated the reaction that so many family members showed when I contacted them about this book. No matter how busy they were, how different their lives had become, or how many years may have passed since the death of the baseball player in their family, they all reacted with genuine joy. It was so wonderful that a total stranger wanted to ensure that their loved one would not ever be forgotten and wanted people to get to know what kind of guy he was.

The moments of happiness I was able to give members of the families, such as Donald Bond, made the work and research that went into this project worthwhile for me. We all want to be remembered for things we do in this life and not have our imprint on the planet washed away like a drawing in the sand when a wave comes in.

That's why it was important for me to write this book. Each reader will take something different from it, but what it is to me is a memorial for lives that should be remembered. That they were baseball players makes the stories interesting. That they were people makes the stories relevant and important.

If you agree, then my job is complete.

INTRODUCTION

With apologies to the long-standing science fiction phenomenon *Star Trek*, death is the final frontier. There is simply no escaping it. Quite often, the end follows a long existence that is the ultimate final chapter in life's best-selling mystery. While the passing of an older person who has lived a full life can cause sadness and tears, nothing rocks our world more than the death of young people, seemingly so long before their time, at least from our way of thinking.

In our culture, athletes almost seem larger than life, invincible as they play their games with joy and vigor. And there are no athletes in our culture who embody such feelings more than baseball players. There are no shoulder pads, and the only time they wear helmets is while they are batting. We get to see them and we get to know them.

Plus, baseball is America's game. Some might attempt to refute that by pointing to the popularity of football, as well as basketball and, in some regions of the country, ice hockey. But baseball is at the core of our country's sports existence. It is the game that we've all played from our early childhood and, quite often, into adulthood. It is also the game that we, to varying degrees, know and understand. Because of that familiarity and comfort level, it is easier to relate to the athletes who play baseball on the professional level than those who play any other sport. We've all done what they're doing, just not nearly as well, thanks in large part to that damn curveball.

The thing that is difficult for many of us to understand is how big leaguers play the game so confidently, so effortlessly. Not only can they wow you with the occasional Ozzie Smith–like acrobatic play, but it's the consistency with which they make the routine plays that most of us find so challenging. After all, if you try long enough, even the typical middle-aged couch potato can make a great play defensively in his softball league—but try making a routine play 10 times in a row. Or, attempt to make contact with a 90-mph fastball. Every now and then a 40- or 50-year-old can close his eyes, swing as hard as he can, and slice a humpback liner into the opposite field. But the odds are those hits will be few and far between.

While they may not be as physically imposing as a gridiron player, the boys of summer have always seemed to be larger than the rest of us, tall and muscular as they played the game under the hot, glistening sun. It's as if they honed their bodies with years of hard, physical work on a farm. In fact, many have. No matter how many years pass, there is still that recurring idea that we could have done some of the same things they do as we watch from the stands or enjoy a game on television. This is the connection that keeps us young and allows our rebirth every spring, as once again we hear the sounds of the smack of the ball in the glove and the crack of the bat as it makes contact with a pitched ball.

It is this connection that keeps us young at heart, even as the years and age lines say we're not so youthful anymore. For when you play sports and have a passion for sports, time can stand still. We remember our favorite players from our childhood and feel young again ourselves.

Sadly, old-timers games and mirrors can cause rude awakenings.

As we enjoy the exploits of our teams and players, they can become larger than life thanks to those Herculean home runs, blazing fastballs, and assembly-line consistency on defense. They seem invincible in so many ways as they play America's game with such elegance that so often the rest of us appear to have two left feet. While time passes, in our minds it stands still. We picture them forever as they were on their fields of dreams. It's as if they'll live forever, coming back to the ballpark again and again, game after game, season after season.

But during the proud history of our game, there have been shocking instances of players who never came back to the park for the next game or the following season. While they might appear larger than life, a baseball player is just a man. None of us can live forever as life, unfortunately, has the ultimate unhitable, 12-to-six curveball that strikes all of us out in the end. Far too often, though, some die young, long before what we feel is their time. It happens to those out of the spotlight and it also happens to those who play America's game.

Shortened Seasons recounts the lives and deaths of baseball players who never made it to the next game. These are players who died with the suddenness and finality of a walk-off home run. For them, there was no next year. For them, there was no next game.

From Hall of Fame players such as Roberto Clemente, Thurman Munson, and Ed Delahanty, to players who were still finding their ultimate niche in the game such as Ken Hubbs, Lyman Bostock, and Darryl Kile, *Shortened Seasons* explores the stories surrounding ballplayers of all categories and abilities who were struck down at the height of their careers.

Some of the stories are shocking, still steeped in mystery. *Shortened Seasons* speaks to the fragile nature of life and just how tentative a gift it truly is. Talented players may seem capable of cheating death as they flaunt their skills on the baseball diamond, but they are just as susceptible as the rest of us when it comes to automobile accidents, plane crashes, life-threatening situations, and lost battles with killer diseases.

Shortened Seasons takes you on an interesting walk through the history of America's game with the final box score for these departed players.

PLAYERS WHO DIED IN AIRCRAFT

F lying is a way of life for the typical professional athlete. Events and games through each season often take them across the country and around the world. While statistics indicate that flying is much safer than driving in a car, that rationalization does little to give solace to those who have lost loved ones, relatives, and friends in airplane crashes.

While this seemingly safe mode of transportation almost always gets passengers to their final destination safe and pretty much on time, there are, of course, examples of tragic crashes that took numerous lives. And unlike automobile accidents, an airplane crash is rarely a fender bender causing minimal damage. Considering the millions of people who fly every year, air travel is absolutely a safe way to get from one destination to the next. By the same token, it has been calculated that approximately 1,200 people die every year in airline-related accidents. Commercial crashes garner most of the headlines, but private planes also crash at an alarming rate.

Various well-known sports figures like boxing champion Rocky Marciano, legendary football coach Knute Rockne, and golfers Champagne Tony Lema and Payne Stewart died in plane crashes.

This chapter recounts the stories of a number of major league baseball players whose lives ended in airplane accidents. Roberto Clemente died in a plane crash while en route to deliver aid to Nicaraguan earthquake victims, and private plane crashes snuffed out the lives of Chicago Cub Kenny Hubbs and Thurman Munson, of the New York Yankees. An outstanding pitching prospect for the San Francisco Giants, Nestor Chavez, was killed in a commercial airline tragedy, and troubled outfielder Len Koenecke of the Brooklyn Dodgers may have attempted one of the first hijackings of an airplane.

Thankfully, one happening that this chapter does not include is a crash involving an entire baseball team. Such tragedies have marred other sports repeatedly. Sixteen members of the Cal Poly-San Luis Obispo football team died in Toledo, Ohio, in October 1960. Four months later, 18 members of the U.S. figure skating team were killed in a plane crash in Belgium.

In a six-week period in the fall of 1970, two college athletic programs were rocked by airplane crashes. Fourteen members of the Wichita State football team died in Colorado on October 2 of that year. Then, in a horrible crash in West Virginia, 37 members of the Marshall University football team were killed.

In December 1977, 14 members of the University of Evansville basketball team, along with coach Bobby Watson, died in Indiana, and in March 1980, the U.S. amateur boxing team lost 14 members in a crash in Poland.

And as recently as 2001, two players and six officials with the Oklahoma State basketball team lost their lives in an airplane crash in Colorado.

People will continue to die in airplane-related accidents, most of them just average people living their lives to the best of their abilities out of the spotlight. But when an athlete or someone famous is killed, it leaves a mark on all of us.

KEN HUBBS

....

Chicago Cubs
Second Base

Bats: Right; Throws: Right
Height: 6 ft. 2 in.; Weight: 175 lbs.

Born: December 23, 1941, in Riverside, Calif.
Died: February 13, 1964, in Provo, Utah, in a plane crash

Signed by the Cubs as an amateur free agent in 1959.
3 Seasons   .247 BA   14 HR   98 RBIs
1962 NL Rookie of the Year
1962 Golden Glove Award Winner

THE ULTIMATE SOPHOMORE JINX

When they were both just young pups in the Chicago Cubs organization, Ken Hubbs and Billy Connors continued to enjoy the friendship that had its beginnings in the 1954 Little League World Series. That year, Connors's Schenectady, N.Y., team defeated Hubbs and his Colton, Calif., team, 7-5, to earn top Little League honors. But the two were both outstanding players who developed not only respect for each other on the baseball field, but a true friendship off the field as well.

In later years both players signed professional contracts with the Chicago Cubs, who had spring training in Arizona. One year when Hubbs was in the Cactus League with the Cubs and Connors was still working out with the minor league squads, Hubbs would fly his private plane over the minor league playing field and cut the engine briefly. This was his special way of acknowledging and waving to his childhood friend. Down on the playing field in the dugout or bullpen, Connors would then wave his warm-up jacket at his pal to acknowledge him. Connors still chuckles over the reaction of teammates who wondered just why in the world he was waving his jacket.

In 1964, Connors and the rest of the baseball world were shocked and saddened to learn that Hubbs, the National League Rookie of the Year in 1962, was killed at the age of 22 when the light plane he was piloting crashed on a frozen lake near Provo, Utah. Also killed in the single-engine Cessna 172 was his friend Dennis Doyle, who was 23 years old.

Hubbs and Doyle were flying to their homes in Colton after participating in a basketball tournament in Provo, which was sponsored by the Church of Jesus Christ of Latter Day Saints. Although he was only 22 years old at the time of his death, Hubbs was considered a mature young man who was very involved with his church and his family.

"I was supposed to go to California with him," said Billy Connors, who pitched in parts of three seasons in the major leagues with the Cubs and the New York Mets. He is now vice president of player personnel for the New York Yankees. "He had just recently gotten his pilot's license and wanted me to go. But I wanted to spend some time at home with my family. They said he had a problem with vertigo, where he thought he was flying level but they were actually going straight down. I lost a helluva friend when that happened.

"He was a team ballplayer. He made a lot of errors but that's partially because he got to more balls than anyone else. Ken was a hardnosed, great athlete who was also a track star, a great basketball player and probably could have been an All-American football player, but he chose baseball. He was such a gifted athlete."

Hubbs, who had obtained his pilot's license two weeks before, got only five miles from the Utah airport en route home to Colton.

According to a report from the National Transportation Safety Board (NTSB), Hubbs exercised poor judgment by continuing a flight into adverse weather conditions. At the time there was a low cloud ceiling and vision was obstructed by blowing snow.

According to Harlan Bement, a Utah aeronautics director, the crash occurred three minutes after Hubbs left Provo Airport in his red and white, single-engine Cessna 172. The pair took off in a snow storm: the plane crashed with great force in a steep spiral nose dive into the lake. Investigators felt it was possible that Hubbs tried to turn around to return to the airport, or simply lost the horizon during the storm, hitting the ice without even realizing his positioning.

It has been reported that it was a fear of flying that convinced Ken Hubbs to take flying lessons in an attempt to put those fears to rest. Other said that he became interested in flying while playing for the Cubs. The team often chartered planes to take them to various cities during the baseball season. It was said that Hubbs would sometimes sit in the cockpit with the pilot, observing and learning.

"I was shocked," said pitcher Morrie Steevens, a teammate on the '62 Cubs. "I couldn't believe when I heard that he had died. He was a young guy who had the world by the tail. I knew he was flying and taking lessons. Ken was a real nice Christian fellow. He was quite religious and a good all-around individual. It was just too bad that his life ended so shortly."

More than 40 years after his death, Billy Connors still remembers the circus catch that Hubbs, with a broken foot, made in that Little League World Series. That World Series included numerous players who would go on to play in the major leagues. In addition to Hubbs and Connors, other future big leaguers included Jim Barbieri, Boog Powell, and Carl "Hawk" Taylor.

Hubbs also started a triple play to end the dreadful 1962 season of the New York Mets, who had the worst team in the history of the game.

After graduating from high school, Hubbs signed a professional contract with the Cubs organization. He hit .298 in 1959 with Morristown of the Appalachian League before slumping to the low .200s the following year split between San Antonio of the Texas League and Lancaster of the Eastern League. But a solid .286 batting average with Wenatchee of the Northwest League in 1961 earned the young infielder a 10-game look-see with the big league club in September. That marked the end of the three-year minor league career of Ken Hubbs. He was now a major league baseball player.

Early in their professional careers, childhood friends Hubbs and Connors were a minor league double-play combination with Hubbs at shortstop and Connors at second base. But Connors, who later became a major league pitcher, was overmatched as an infielder at the professional level. He was sent to develop his pitching skills and Hubbs was switched to second base. His ascent to the big leagues was underway.

During his rookie campaign in the majors, Hubbs made quite a splash. He hit a respectable .260 and played a strong second base, setting records by going 78 consecutive games without an error and handling 418 total chances. This broke not only the National League fielding mark set by Red Schoendiest, but also the major league record set by Bobby Doerr. Hubbs won the National League Rookie of the Year honors, and became the first recipient of that award to also win a Gold Glove Award. Ken Hubbs was the real deal.

"In my opinion, had he lived he would have become one of the all-time greats of the game," said Connors. "He was a tall, lanky kid who could do it all."

Baseball is a game that can bring glory in one respect and bring reality in another. Hubbs also led the league in two areas that he certainly could have done without. He struck out 129 times and grounded into 20 double plays batting second in the Cubs lineup behind speedy leadoff man Lou Brock.

"We played together in the instructional league in Arizona and in '62 in the major leagues," said Steevens. "He was quite a good basketball player and football player too. But he chose baseball. Ken was a good ballplayer, a good fielder, and a better than average hitter. But he was just an A-One fellow. I wish he could have lived out his career and his life. It's a shame."

In his sophomore year, Hubbs knocked 37 strikeouts off of his total from the year before, but the 1963 campaign also saw his average fall to .235. But regardless of the outcome, from his first big league game to his last, on September 29, 1963, Hubbs played with heart, determination, and hustle. And, by all accounts, he was not just a fine ballplayer, but also an outstanding human being.

Many years after his death, Hubbs is remembered throughout the baseball community as a player whose legacy will always be incomplete. But in his home town of Colton, Calif., he is still revered and remembered. Colton High School has a gym named after him, which displays his many trophies and other memorabilia. The Ken Hubbs' Little League was also renamed to honor its fallen hero.

One year Hubbs was the Rookie of the Year in the National League with a future that seemingly had few limitations. Just a year later, he suffered the ultimate sophomore jinx when his life was cut tragically short.

"It's just a shame because he had such a bright future," said Connors. "We spent a lot of time together in the instructional league and in spring training. I just miss being around him."

Hubbs's uniform number 16 was retired by the club and 2,000 people attended his funeral in Colton, Calif. Pallbearers at his funeral were his manager Bob Kennedy and teammates Glen Hobbie, Don Elston, Ron Santo, Ernie Banks, and Dick Ellsworth.

THURMAN MUNSON

New York Yankees
Catcher

Bats: Right; Throws: Right
Height: 5 ft. 11 in.; Weight: 194 lbs.

Born: June 7, 1947, in Akron, Ohio
Died: August 2, 1979, in Canton, Ohio, in a private airplane crash

Drafted by the Yankees in the first round of the 1968 Amateur
   Draft.
11 Seasons   .292 BA   113 HR   701 RBIs
Seven-time All Star
1970 Rookie of the Year
1976 American League MVP
Three Golden Gloves

THE PRIDE OF THE YANKEES

Whether a Yankee supporter or not, any baseball fan with even a
pedestrian knowledge of America's Pastime in the 1970s knew about
Thurman Munson. The backstop for the Bronx Bombers was considered to be the leader of the team and as a result was named the
first Yankee captain since Lou Gehrig.

   On the field he looked like the ultimate baseball warrior, sporting a five o'clock shadow, a burly mustache, and a seemingly grumpy

mood. But he was an outstanding catcher who was well-respected for his ability to call a game and handle a pitching staff. At the plate, he was a clutch performer who also could hit for power and average. Suffice to say that on the ball field and in the clubhouse Thurman Munson was the leader of the New York Yankees.

The first-round draft pick of the Yankees in the 1968 amateur draft, Munson quickly became a force on the big league team. He broke in with Binghamton of the Eastern League and hit .301 as a 21-year-old catcher. The following season, 1969, Munson left the minor leagues for good after hitting .363 in 28 games at Syracuse in the International League. He made his big league debut with the Yankees that summer, hitting .349 in limited duty. By the time 1970 rolled around, Munson was the Yankees everyday catcher. And he was up to the task, hitting .302 with six homers and 53 RBIs in 132 games.

Munson's career was clearly taking off. He was an All-Star in 1971 and from 1973 until 1978. He was chosen AL Rookie of the Year in 1970 and won Gold Glove Awards in 1973 and 1975. Munson was the American League's Most Valuable Player hitting .302 with 17 homers and 105 RBIs in 1976 en route to a trip to the World Series and a loss to the Cincinnati Reds.

"He was a winning ballplayer," said Munson's close friend and teammate Bobby Murcer. "I've been in baseball for 41 years and have seen players who have good years with statistics who just don't know how to win. Other players have the good numbers but know how to win. He was that type of player.

"Being a winning ballplayer has a lot to do with their makeup, how they perceive the game. Are they interested in individual achievement or team achievement?

"On the field, the game dictates what you need to do. You have to recognize it. A lot of guys just don't do what the situation dictates, like swinging for a home run when they should move the runner over."

Munson's offensive statistics and clutch performances are the stuff of legend at Yankee Stadium. But another aspect of his professionalism was probably not recognized by most fans.

"He ran a pitching staff as good as any catcher I'd ever seen," said Murcer. "He took the pressure off the pitching staff because they believed in him. No matter what he put down and called for, they just believed in him and threw the pitch. It kept them from thinking and you're better off when you keep a pitcher from thinking. They could just relax and throw the ball."

Off the playing field, "Thurm," as so many friends and teammates called him, was a loving husband and a devoted father who wanted to spend as much time as possible with his wife, Diana, and their three children, Tracy, Kelly, and Michael. In fact it was his desire to be closer to his family and their Ohio home during the baseball season that first got Munson interested in flying.

The family had tried living near New York, but the burly receiver just was not a big city guy. He was just a guy who was comfortable in knock-around clothes with no socks and a good cigar in his mouth. While he played like he belonged in the big city, in his heart where he longed to be was with Diana and the kids.

Not only was Thurman Munson a respected and well-liked member of the Yankees, but he was appreciated and respected by opponents as well as teammates. In spite of the age-old rivalry between the Yankees and the Boston Red Sox, infielder Rick Burleson was a big fan of the Yankees backstop.

"He was one of my all-time favorites," Burleson said of No. 15. "He was so reliable, the leader and the captain of the team. I just had so much respect for the way he went about the game; his professionalism and clutchness. The way he carried himself. Competing against a guy like that, it's hard not to like the guy. We both played the game hard.

"I love to tell the story about the time the Yankees came to play us in Winter Haven, where the Red Sox had spring training. I had asked our manager, Don Zimmer, if I could try to steal bases on my own during the spring. I thought I could help out the club by stealing a few bags and during spring training was something like eight-for-eight.

"The Yankees came in and I got two bags on Munson that day. Later during the regular season, he came into second base and knocked the Hell out of me on a double play.

"When I came up to bat, he looked up and said to me, 'Hey Rooster, we're even now.'

"I asked him what he was talking about and he mentioned that spring training game where I ran on him and embarrassed him by stealing two bases. He never forgot that I did that and had to let me know about it. I just loved the guy."

Had Thurman Munson lived, he could very well have become a major league coach or manager. Or, because of his love of family and Canton, he may just have hung 'em up and invested in real estate. Sadly, what could have happened was not to be, as fate threw the ultimate knockdown pitch at the Yankee captain.

As the 1979 season got underway, Munson's love of flying continued to be a big factor in his life. After flying for 18 months, he purchased his third plane. Unlike his previous propeller-driven aircraft, his new $1.4 million Cessna CE-501 was a jet-powered plane, which was considerably more powerful than the planes he was used to flying.

Enjoying a day off in Ohio on August 2, 1979, and planning to meet the family for dinner, Munson went to the airport and was sitting in his new plane with flight instructor David Hall and a new business partner, Jerry Anderson. The three decided to go for a ride in the Cessna, which would also give Munson an opportunity to practice touch-and-go landings.

At just after 4 P.M. on that fateful afternoon, the plane crashed about 600 feet short of runway 19 at the Akron-Canton Airport. Both Hall and Anderson were injured in the crash. Munson was pinned between the instrument panel and his seat when a fire broke out in the wreckage of the aircraft. Both Hall and Anderson attempted to free Munson, but were unable to do so. The two were able to escape from the plane but were forced to leave the Yankee captain behind.

According to the NTSB, the probable cause of the accident was Munson's failure to maintain sufficient airspeed and to recognize the need for timely and sufficient power application to prevent a stall during approach to the airport.

That evening as baseball games were played throughout America, news of the tragic death of Thurman Munson spread across the baseball world. Was the new Cessna too much plane for him, or was it simply a tragic accident?

"He was obviously a competent pilot going from a Piper Cub to a jet," said Bobby Murcer. "Maybe he just didn't have enough time in the plane to realize that it would stall out at a certain speed. But he was very passionate about flying and really loved it. He died doing something he really enjoyed."

It was clear that Munson enjoyed himself no matter where he was, with his family, flying a plane, or being with fellow ballplayers. He was a good friend and a loyal teammate. At the same time, he was also very guarded with people, particularly members of the press corps.

"If Thurman was your friend, you'd never have a better one," said Murcer. "He was a loyal guy who loved his family and loved being in Canton. But he seemed to want to protect the perimeter around him. He could be rough with people who didn't know him, but I never experienced that. I still remember all the times that he, Gene Michael, Mel Stottlemyre, and I would play cards, kind of a high-low poker game. We had a lot of fun together."

Not only were the Yankees a lesser organization after his tragic death, but his loss was felt throughout the rest of baseball.

"When he passed I just felt horrible," said Rick Burleson. "With him gone, that rivalry between the Yankees and the Red Sox wasn't what it was before. It went away for a while and you'd see guys from opposing teams talking in the outfield before the game. That didn't happen before."

It seems reasonable to assume Munson would have been groomed to play more at first base and the outfield than behind the plate as the rigors of catching had taken their toll on him. But he was a productive player up to his last game.

ROBERTO CLEMENTE

Pittsburgh Pirates
Right Field

Bats: Right; Throws: Right
Height: 5 ft. 11 in.; Weight: 175 lbs.

Born: August 18, 1934, in Carolina, Puerto Rico
Died: December 31, 1972, in a plane crash at sea

Drafted by Pittsburgh from the Brooklyn Dodgers in the 1954
   Rule V draft.
18 Seasons   .317 BA   240 HR   1,305 RBIs
12-time All Star
1966 NL Most Valuable Player
12 Gold Gloves
4 Batting Titles

AS GOOD AS IT GETS

Millions of baseball fans awoke on New Year's Day 1973 to the worst
hangover they could ever imagine. After ringing in the New Year just
hours before, word spread of the New Year's Eve death of Pittsburgh
Pirates great Roberto Clemente. The All Star right fielder and four
others were killed when the plane in which they were flying supplies
to help survivors hit by a severe earthquake in Managua, Nicaragua,

two days before Christmas, crashed into the ocean about a mile off of the Puerto Rican coast.

The NTSB cited numerous problems with the engine and upkeep of the aircraft as the primary cause of the crash. Shock and dismay replaced the joy with which the Pirates ended their regular season when on September 30, 1972, the 38-year-old smashed the 3,000th hit of his remarkable career, a double against southpaw Jon Matlack of the New York Mets. Surely Clemente had at least a couple more years left in his career. He hit .312 in his final season, and while slowed by some injuries, he remained a force to be reckoned with.

The Pirates made the playoffs that year, but lost in five games to the Cincinnati Reds. In the National League Championship Series, Clemente hit just .235, garnering four hits in 17 at bats.

From the dog days of summer and a pennant race to a milestone hit in a wonderful career on the baseball field exemplified by the 1972 campaign were not all that defined Clemente. His dedication to being a positive role model was also exemplified by his willingness to participate in charitable functions, to sign thousands of autographs, and put his life on the line to aid earthquake survivors on a New Year's Eve that would go down in infamy in the minds and hearts of baseball fans.

"It was just a total shock," said Clemente's teammate and friend, pitcher Steve Blass. "We were at a party and got a call. We went to Puerto Rico for a memorial service and I read a eulogy. The accident was just a mismatch of unfortunate equipment that was not cared for and maintained. Just a tragic combination of negative things.

"Clemente was such a gifted player. He played at a level that was a little bit above the average major leaguer. He had his own personal level, above the fray. It was great fun to watch him play because he was so gifted. You didn't want to miss watching him play the game. He could turn a 10-year veteran into a 10-year-old kid.

"You remember the way he carried himself as a person, with such character. He just exuded dignity. He was a wonderfully gifted player who carried himself at a little higher plane than the rest of us. He had such poise. If we were good baseball soldiers, he was a good baseball general."

His ability and professionalism made an impression on all those who knew him. The person they knew off the field and in the clubhouse was special to each.

"I played with Roberto for five years," said Jim Pagliaroni, a catcher who spent 11 seasons in the major leagues. "In my estimation, he was the second best ballplayer I've ever seen in my life after Willie Mays. He was a wonderful human being, a lot of fun to be around. He was a practical joker and a real team leader.

"When there were reporters around, he had his business face on. Roberto knew what he meant to the people of Puerto Rico. He could have been elected Mayor there. He always was aware of his image there that he wanted to be very positive, a good role model. Much like Willie Stargell, he never played the victim and never made excuses."

Roberto Clemente had a style all his own. He didn't need a Pittsburgh Pirates uniform with number 21 on the back to be recognizable. His batting stance, running style, and basket catches on routine fly balls made Clemente easy to spot.

"He looked unorthodox at the plate sometimes," said Blass, who has broadcast Pirates games since 1986. "And he didn't run, he galloped. Every aspect of his game was fun to watch. He never looked fluid or graceful, but there was no pitch he couldn't reach.

"One time I came up to Roberto in the clubhouse and told him that if I was ever traded that I'd be able to get him out. All the other pitchers pitch him away and he'd hit .360. I said that I would pitch him inside. He smiled and said, 'If you pitch me inside, I will hit the ball to Harrisburg.'"

Originally signed by the Brooklyn Dodgers, this native of Puerto Rico was drafted by the Pirates in the minor league draft for $4,000 on November 22, 1954. Clemente had hit just .257 for the Dodgers top farm team in Montreal in 1954, but he was a five-tool player who could do it all.

While his rookie campaign with the Pirates in 1955 was not one of his best seasons, the 20-year-old did hit .255 in 124 games with five home runs. On the field he had a .978 fielding percentage gunning down 18 base runners during the season. While not a superstar early in his big league career, Clemente showed steady improvement as did the Pittsburgh team.

While he hit .311 in his sophomore year, the rifle-armed outfielder then hit .253 in 1957 before improving to .289 in 1958, and .296 in 1959. In 1960, Clemente served notice once and for all that he was the real deal hitting .314 with 16 homers and 94 RBIs, good enough to earn him the first of what would ultimately be 14 All Star appearances. But more important for the team, the Pirates won the National League pennant and went on to defeat the New York Yankees in the World Series when Bill Mazeroski smacked a home run off Ralph Terry in the ninth inning of the seventh and final game.

Clemente hit safely in every game of the Fall Classic, finishing up with a solid .310 average. His steady improvement as a major league player saw his first .300 season in 1960 represent the first of what were to be eight consecutive .300 campaigns and a total of 11 out of 12.

However, that season also saw Clemente react unhappily to finishing eighth in the MVP vote that was won by his teammate Dick Groat. Though he was the Bucs top run producer that year, he felt snubbed by the voting. As a result, he never wore his championship ring, opting to don his All Star ring.

There would be no stopping Roberto Clemente after that. The success he enjoyed in 1960 only increased the following season when he won the first of his four batting championships with an impressive .351 average, and 23 home runs. Just six seasons before, his average was nearly 100 points lower.

He continued to make his mark known winning back-to-back batting titles in 1964 and 1965, hitting .339 and .329 respectively. And then in 1967, Clemente enjoyed his career best average of .357 to capture batting honors once more.

In addition to his stellar performance on the playing field, Roberto Clemente was a quiet leader in the clubhouse who led by his extraordinary example.

"When I first came up to the Pirates, I didn't want him to look down on me," said Steve Blass. "I felt that I had to validate myself to him to prove I belonged. He was a quiet guy who kept very much to himself. He was not an idle chatter kind of guy. But I always found myself trying to impress him."

While no one could doubt his effort on the playing field, some considered him a complainer and a borderline hypochondriac because of continued physical ailments. But he continued to play every day in spite of a painful back injury in 1954, an arm injury five years later, and contracting malaria in 1965.

Clemente bristled at the suggestion that he was brittle. As he was known to say, "You think I'm a hypochondriac? A hypochondriac cannot produce. I produce."

There was no doubt of that. Through injury and illness, Clemente continued to play and play well for the Pirates climaxing in 1966 when he won the Most Valuable Player Award on the heels of the season in which he hit .317, with a career high of 29 home runs and 119 RBIs for the third-place Pirates. His toughest competition for the National League Award was second-place finisher Sandy Koufax of the Los Angeles Dodgers, who had a 27-9 record with a 1.73 ERA.

Clemente continued to excel on the field over the next few seasons that included a league-leading .357 average in 1967 and hitting at a .345 clip in 1969.

The 1970 team made it to the postseason for the first time in a decade as their All Star right fielder led the way with a .352 batting average. But tough pitching and timely hitting helped the Cincinnati Reds defeat Pittsburgh in three games to advance to the World Series.

But the die was cast as the Pirates came back in 1971 to once again dominate and capture the Eastern Division crown led by the likes of Clemente, who hit .341 with 86 RBIs. He hit .333 in the NLCS that saw the Pirates defeat the San Francisco Giants in four games, and he then smacked the baseball at a .414 clip in the heart-stopping seven-game World Series victory against the Baltimore Orioles.

"He was the MVP in the World Series and I had a great one as well, with a couple of complete games," said Steve Blass. "I'll never forget flying back to Pittsburgh after the last game. He got out of his seat and came up to me and asked me to stand up. He said, 'Let me embrace you,' and gave me a big hug."

In what turned out to be his final season in 1972, at the age of 37, Clemente was limited to 102 games due to nagging injuries, but he still hit .312, once again helping the Pirates return to the postseason for the third consecutive year. But the magic of the World Championship in 1971 ended as the Reds once again beat Pittsburgh in a five-game NLCS. In the final action of his career, Clemente hit .235 in the series with four hits in 17 at bats.

Clemente's game typically rose to new levels at clutch time as he hit .318 in five postseason series, including .362 in his two World Series appearances.

The shock and disbelief over his sudden passing became all too real just a couple of months later when the Pirates reported to spring training in Bradenton, Fla. Clemente, who had been a major part of the team, on the field and off, was missing.

"The real impact on the baseball season was at spring training when Roberto wasn't there," said Blass. "Everybody was there but Roberto. Then it really hit hard for the team as a whole. That's when it really hit everyone.

"He was a friend and a wonderful teammate. There was a closeness as a teammate and a closeness as a friend. We were solid friends and very solid teammates. I lost a great teammate and friend."

Both on the playing field and off, Roberto Clemente was the total package. So much so that just 11 weeks following his tragic death, the Baseball Writers Association of America waved the mandatory five-year waiting period and elected him to the Hall of Fame with his name on 93 percent of the ballots.

NESTOR CHAVEZ

San Francisco Giants
Pitcher

Bats: Right; Throws: Right
Height: 6 ft.; Weight: 170 lbs.

Born: July 6, 1947, in Chacao, Venezuela
Died: March 16, 1969, in Maracaibo, Venezuela

Signed as an amateur free agent by the San Francisco Giants
  before the 1964 season.
1 Season   1 Win   0 Losses   0.00 ERA

DIED IN A HORRIFIC CRASH

The news reports were no different than similar ones that might be
filling the airwaves and newspapers today. Viasa Airline Flight No.
742 from Grano de Oro Airport in Maracaibo, Venezuela, en route
to Miami, crashed into a heavily populated suburban area killing 154
people, 84 on the airliner and 70 on the ground.

That the tragedy occurred nearly 40 years ago does not lessen the
pain of what was, at the time, the worst airline disaster in Venezuelan
history. Takeoff calculations were based on erroneous information and
there were faulty temperature sensors along the runway. As the DC-9
lumbered down the runway and took off, it struck electrical power
lines. Two minutes later, it crashed into homes, buses, cars, and trucks,
spewing blazing fuel over a five-block area. Seven houses immediately

burst into flames. Five members of a family were killed as they sat at their dinner table. Witnesses said that the plane appeared to have exploded in flight just before hitting the ground.

Then, as now, such reports send a shiver up our spines as most people have traveled in airplanes, or have loved ones who do so. Many lives were lost in this horrific crash in the spring of 1969. One of the young lives snuffed out was a young pitcher in the San Francisco Giants organization, Nestor Chavez.

The hard-throwing right-hander was signed by the Giants prior to the start of the 1964 season after he compiled a 34-3 record at Miranda State College in Venezuela. Chavez was nicknamed "Latigo," or "The Whip," in his homeland because of his outstanding fastball.

Considered a top prospect in the Giants organization, Chavez had a 47-20 minor league record in the Giants farm system by the time he was recalled by the parent club toward the end of the 1967 season. The 19-year-old pitched in just two games, but served notice that he was everything that the organization hoped he would be—and more.

In his final major league game, Chavez was the winning pitcher in the Giants 1-0 victory over the Philadelphia Phillies in the second game of a double-header. Southpaw Ray Sedecki beat the Phillies in the first game of the twin bill and Bill Henry, Chavez, and Lindy McDaniel shut down the high-powered Philadelphia offense in the night cap.

After Henry threw three scoreless innings, "Latigo" entered the game and threw four scoreless innings, surrendering just two hits and two walks, while striking out two. The Giants took a 1-0 lead with him in the game, which was saved for the young right-hander by McDaniel, who threw two shutout innings.

Chavez finished the year 1-0 with a 0.00 ERA. The young phenomenon needed shoulder surgery after the season, which sidelined him for more than a year. But in March 1969, he was on his way to rehab his shoulder in the minor leagues with the hope of once again having the chance to show his stuff on the major league level.

But then at the age of 21, Nestor Chavez boarded that ill-fated flight for Miami.

LEN KOENECKE

Brooklyn Dodgers
Center Field

Bats: Left; Throws: Right
Height: 5 ft. 11 in.;
  Weight: 180 lbs.

Courtesy of the Baseball Hall of Fame.

Born: January 18, 1904, in
  Baraboo, Wis.
Died: September 17, 1935, in Toronto, Canada

Purchased by the Brooklyn Dodgers on June 20, 1933.
3 Seasons   .297 BA   22 HR   114 RBIs   11 SB

AN EARLY HIJACKER?

Judging by the season he enjoyed with the Brooklyn Dodgers in 1934, it seemed as if the sky was the limit for the 30-year-old center fielder getting his second shot at the major leagues. Playing in 123 games, Len Koenecke hit an impressive .320 with 14 home runs and 73 RBIs. Two years previous, he had played in 42 games for the New York Giants, with a .255 average.

The powerfully built left-handed hitter appeared to be ready to continue as a regular with Casey Stengel's Dodgers. And as the 1935 campaign got underway, Koenecke was once again patrolling the outfield.

But his production sagged as did his attitude. Discipline problems ensued and although he was still hitting .283, on September 16, the star outfielder of the previous season was sent home for the balance of the season, his future in baseball questionable at best. But the events of Tuesday, September 17, represent one of the strangest happenings in the history of the game that saw Koenecke beaten to death with a fire extinguisher on a private plane he had chartered.

Was he one of the first hijackers to attempt to take the controls of an airplane while in flight, or was he just someone who got out of hand after drowning his sorrows over the potential end of his major league career? While the answer to that question will never be known for certain, the events of that evening will go down in history as one of the most puzzling nights baseball has had to endure.

After being told to go home for the rest of the season by Stengel, Koenecke proceeded to get drunk. While he was on board an American Airlines flight from Chicago to Newark, with a stopover in Detroit, things started to get out of hand. Shortly after takeoff from Chicago, a stewardess noticed that the ballplayer had carried a bottle of liquor onto the flight. A short time later, Koenecke was out of his seat arguing with another passenger. As the stewardess tried to see what the problem was, Koenecke hit her and knocked her down.

After the copilot of the plane succeeded in calming him down, a short time later, he was causing yet another disturbance. When the plane landed in Detroit, the seemingly intoxicated Koenecke was ejected and not allowed to continue on the regularly scheduled flight to Newark. At that time, he chartered a plane to Buffalo, where he had enjoyed success in the minor leagues and had friends. The pilot of the plane, William J. Mulqueeney, and his friend, Irwin Davis, found themselves in a dangerous situation shortly after the flight got underway.

Not long after takeoff, Koenecke was at it again, poking the pilot repeatedly as he tried to fly the aircraft and reportedly tried to take control of the plane. Davis then attempted to calm the ballplayer, but Koenecke hit him and the two began to fight on the floor of the plane, which Mulqueeney was having a difficult time controlling because of the melee on board.

As the enraged ballplayer fought with Davis, he also tried to engage the pilot. Holding the controls with one hand, Mulqueeney picked up a fire extinguisher and hit Koenecke a number of times until he stopped fighting.

"I had to come to a decision," Mulqueeney told a constable of New Toronto, a Toronto suburb, as was reported by the *New York Times*. "It was either a case of the three of us crashing or doing something to Koenecke. I watched my chance, grabbed the fire extinguisher and walloped him over the head.

"With the passenger quiet, I took a look around, saw the open field and came down. If he's dead, I'm the one that killed him. My God, I wish I could take those blows back." So shaken was the pilot over the incident that he landed the plane at Long Branch race track, in Toronto.

The autopsy surgeon, Dr. W. H. Taylor of New Toronto, said the cause of Koenecke's death was a brain hemorrhage and that his face was severely battered.

Both Mulqueeney and Davis were booked for manslaughter. At an inquest, an attorney for Mulqueeney said that he felt Koenecke was deliberately attempting to commit suicide. The manslaughter charges were dismissed on September 20 when Magistrate Douglas Keith ruled that the two acted in self-defense.

Koenecke's trek to the major leagues began in 1931 when his contract was purchased by John McGraw, manager of the New York Giants. After starting the 1932 season with the big club, he was sent to Jersey City, where he hit an impressive .355.

After a fine season with Buffalo in 1933, he was acquired by the Dodgers organization, which no doubt thought that the center fielder would be a centerpiece of their team for years. In addition to his .320 batting average in 1934, Koenecke set a National League record with a fielding average of .994, committing just two errors while handling 310 put outs. He also added six assists.

In his final major league appearance on September 15, 1935, Len Koenecke grounded out as a pinch hitter at Chicago.

When told of his death, many of his Dodger teammates cried and the entire team wore black armbands in memory of Koenecke.

In the days the followed the tragedy, officials of the Federal Bureau of Air Commerce met and concluded that the pilot of an airplane is the "Czar" of the plane, the person solely in charge, as long as the plane is in the air. They also ruled that jurisdiction of any crime that occurs on board a plane would belong to the city or town the plane was flying over when the event occurred.

MARV GOODWIN

Cincinnati Reds
Pitcher

Bats: Right; Throws: Right
Height: 5 ft. 11 in.; Weight: 168 lbs.

Born: January 16, 1891, in Gordonsville, Va.
Died: October 21, 1925, in Houston, Tex.

7 Seasons   21 Wins   25 Losses   3.30 ERA

A TRAINING FLIGHT
GONE BAD

Marvin Mardo Goodwin was one of the fortunate pitchers who was registered as eligible to continue to throw the spitball after the pitch was deemed illegal since it was a major part of his game.

Breaking in with Washington in 1916, the slightly built right-hander pitched in three games without a decision. The following season, the 26-year-old hitched on with St. Louis, where he became a familiar figure on the pitcher's mound, logging a 6-4 record in 14 appearances with a very respectable 2.21 ERA.

After not pitching in the major leagues in 1918, Goodwin had his best year in 1919, winning 11 and losing 9 in 33 games. He was a spot starter, getting the nod 17 times and finished the season with a 2.51 ERA. But over the next three seasons, he was just 4-10 with St. Louis.

After spending two seasons in the minor leagues, Goodwin resurfaced with the Cincinnati Reds in 1925 going 0-2 in four outings. His final appearance was on October 4.

Just more than three months later, he was killed at the age of 34 when, as a member of the Army Air Corps, he crashed his plane on a training flight.

Tom Gastall

Courtesy of Boston University.

Baltimore Orioles
Catcher

Bats: Right; Throws: Right
Height: 6 ft. 2 in.;
    Weight: 187 lbs.

Born: June 13, 1932,
    in Fall River, Mass.
Died: September 20, 1956, in Riviera Beach, Md.

Signed as a bonus baby amateur free agent by the Baltimore
    Orioles on June 20, 1955.
2 Seasons   .181 BA   0 HR   4 RBIs

A GIFTED ATHLETE WHO CHOSE BASEBALL

Along with his teammate, the legendary Harry Agganis, Tom Gastall
has gone down in the annals of Boston University sports history.
Inducted into the BU Hall of Fame in 1959, Gastall was named the
1955 Boston University Athlete of the Year. He was captain of the
baseball and basketball teams as well as the starting quarterback on
the football team. In fact, he led the gridiron squad to a 7-2 record.

Such stellar performances on the football field were nothing new to Gastall. During his high school career at Durfee High School in Fall River, he quarterbacked the football team, was a star rebounder and playmaker on the hardwood of the basketball court, and may have been the best baseball player in the league.

As a senior signal caller, Gastall tied Agganis's record of throwing four touchdown passes in a single game. He also tossed a 96-yard touchdown pass that season. Not too shabby for a player who was shifted from quarterback to playing end as a freshman to accommodate Agganis, who returned to school following his discharge from the Marines.

Gastall continued his three-sport mastery at BU, earning 12 letters, four each for baseball, basketball, and football. From as early as his sophomore year, professional baseball scouts from as many as 14 teams covered his games. Making that fact even more impressive is that in the 1950s, there were only 16 major league teams. He turned down a number of offers to play professional baseball opting to stay in school and earn his degree.

Much like his college teammate Agganis, Gastall was chosen in the National Football League draft. But rather than sign with the Detroit Lions, this Fall River, Mass., native chose his true love, baseball, and was signed to reported $40,000 bonus by the Baltimore Orioles in June 1955.

"His goal was to be a major league baseball player," said his son Tom Gastall, who is an elementary school principal. "It's what he wanted to be and he stuck with it. I was very young when he died, I didn't really feel the loss until I got older. From everything I've ever heard, he was basically just a good guy. It's nice hearing people say that he was a good guy and such a good ballplayer. People kind of revered him as a ballplayer and that's always been a source of pride for me. I've also been told that he was really nice to kids and would play ball with them."

Gastall played in a time when "bonus baby" players were forced to stay on the major league roster for two years. After joining the Orioles in 1955, Gastall appeared in just 20 games, getting four hits in 27 at bats for a meager .148 average. In 1956, he began to see a little more action, hitting .196 in 32 games through September 19 of that year.

"He came right out of college and had to stay with the Orioles because he was a bonus baby," said Gus Triandos, who was the starting catcher with Baltimore for most of the 1950s. "Tom was a real nice guy who kind of kept to himself. I guess you could say he was a loner.

"He never played very much, but he was always anxious to learn. I kind of felt that he made a mistake by signing with the Orioles since we played in a big ballpark. He didn't have a lot of power and might have been better off signing with a club that had a smaller park. He wanted to play winter ball and wanted to get his pilot's license so he could fly to South America after the season and play. Plus I think he wanted to fly back home to Fall River when the season ended."

Gastall always had an interest in flying and had been in the Air Force ROTC in school. He decided to take advantage of an off day in the Orioles schedule on September 20 to make a flight in a small private plane to qualify for his pilot's license. After an early practice he and Triandos drove home together and Gastall spoke of his plans to take advantage of the time off to fly.

He had actually earned his student pilot's license and had garnered about 20 hours of solo time when he took off in his single-engine Ercoupe at about 6 P.M. from an airport in Easton, Md. About 15 minutes after takeoff, he radioed that he was having trouble and planned to crash land his plane into Chesapeake Bay. Apparently, his engine had failed over the Bay.

Five days later, one day after officials called off a search for the young catcher, his body was found floating just offshore in Chesapeake Bay. He was identified by his Boston University ring with his initials, TEG, inscribed.

He left a wife, Rosemary, and his son, Thomas Michael, who was 15 months old at the time of his death. Also left behind were tens of thousands of fans who remembered his exploits in high school and college who hoped to see him make headlines with his exploits on the field with the Baltimore Orioles. But, sadly, the final headlines he made had to do with his tragic death.

CHARLIE "MULE" PEETE

St. Louis Cardinals
Outfielder

Bats: Left; Throws: Right
Height: 5 ft. 9 in.; Weight: 190 lbs.

Born: February 22, 1929, in Franklin, Va.
Died: November 27, 1956, in Caracas, Venezuela

Drafted by the St. Louis Cardinals from Portsmouth in the
   1954 minor league draft.
1 Season   .192 BA   0 HR   6 RBIs

POTENTIAL THAT NEVER
REACHED ITS FRUITION

A veteran of the Negro Leagues, Charlie "Mule" Peete was expected
to be the first starting black baseball player with the St. Louis
Cardinals. But after two solid minor league seasons in the St. Louis
organization with Omaha, Peete played in just 23 games for the
Cards in 1956 before tragedy struck.

Following the season in an attempt to hone his skills even further
for a real run at a starting position in the St. Louis outfield in 1957,
Peete was traveling to play winter-league ball in Venezuela. The plane
in which he was flying crashed into a 6,700-foot mountain while on
approach to the airport in Cevilla. Officials found that the pilot didn't

follow normal approach procedures in this tragic accident that killed all 25 people on board. Adding even more sorrow to the event is that Peete's wife and three children were also killed in the crash.

So ended his trek that so many felt would end up with him starting with the Cardinals. After the team drafted him from Portsmouth in November 1954, Charlie Peete was sent to the Omaha Cardinals of the American Association. He hit a solid .317 in 99 games in 1955, which was only an appetizer of things to come.

In 1956, Peete came of age. The 27-year-old returned to Omaha where he led the league in hitting with a stellar .350 average, adding 16 home runs. He no doubt had the minor league qualifications to compete on the major league level. The only question about his ability was what some scouts considered to be an awkward batting stance. Like many other hitters, he also appeared to have a weakness for curveballs thrown low-and-away near the outside corner of the plate.

Following his breakout season in Omaha, Peete was recalled to St. Louis, where he played in 23 games with a .192 average in 52 at bats. While he did not hit a major league home run, the burly outfielder did connect for a two doubles and a pair of triples.

But his path to a long major league career was interrupted by the tragic flight that crashed into a Venezuela mountain.

CORY LIDLE

Courtesy of the Philadelphia Phillies.

New York Yankees
Pitcher

Bats: Right; Throws: Right
Height: 5 ft. 11 in.; Weight:
   190 lbs.
Born: March 22, 1972,
   in Hollywood, Calif.
Died: October 11, 2006,
   in New York

Acquired from the Philadelphia Phillies with Bobby Abreu
   for Matt Smith, Jesus Sanchez, C. J. Henry, and Carlos
   Monastrios.
9 Seasons   82 Wins   72 Losses   2 Saves   4.57 ERA

PITCHER'S DEATH A FLASHBACK
TO SEPTEMBER 11 ATTACKS

It was a typical busy day in New York City. The hustle and bustle of
the Big Apple was apparent throughout Manhattan, including the fash-
ionable Upper East Side. But at 2:42 on the afternoon of Wednesday,
October 11, 2006, fear and panic quickly spread from New York across
an entire country.

A small plane had smashed into the 30th floor of the Belaire
building, a 42-story residential high rise located at 524 E. 72nd

Street. Shocked witnesses saw a horrific fiery crash that had an eerie resemblance to the terrorist attacks on the World Trade Center on September 11, 2001. In fact, as television networks began live coverage of the incident all across the country, there were no immediate assurances that this was not part of yet another terrorist attack.

Within minutes, the Pentagon scrambled fighter jets over numerous major cities and FBI counterterrorism squads were dispatched to the scene of the crash. But as flames and smoke continued to billow out from the skyscraper, it became known that the plane that crashed into the building was owned by New York Yankees pitcher, Cory Lidle.

It soon became apparent that the crash was not part of another terrorist plot, but a tragic accident that killed Lidle, 34, and his flight instructor, Tyler Stanger, 26. Not only was the crash reminiscent of the September 11 attacks, but it also rang a sad and familiar tone with New York Yankee fans who still remember the tragic death of catcher and team captain Thurman Munson, who also died in a private plane he was piloting on August 2, 1979, at the Akron-Canton Airport.

Cory Lidle was a nine-year major league veteran who boasted an 82-72 career record accumulated with seven teams. While not a top-of-the-rotation type of pitcher, the right-hander was a competent and dependable third or fourth starter in a major league rotation. In his final season, 2006, he had a 12-10 mark split between the Philadelphia Phillies and the New York Yankees. It was the fifth time in his career that Lidle had won at least 12 games in a season.

That was quite an accomplishment considering the fact that Lidle never lit up the radar gun with his fastball. His stuff was mediocre and the sum of his pitching parts did not equal the finished product. Cory Lidle was a fierce competitor who prepared for each game, knew his strengths and weaknesses, and never let the hitter off the hook.

"When he got involved with something, pitching or whatever, he was very conscientious," said Rich Dubee, his pitching coach with the Philadelphia Phillies. "If he had a passion, he took a lot of pride in being the best he could be. Cory maximized everything out of his ability. He took pride in his professionalism and was a very good competitor.

"We got along just fine and even played golf together. When we put together a game plan, we pretty much were together on it. He was very dedicated and not stubborn at all. Cory was the type of guy who did what he had to do to win. That being said, if things were happening late in a game he was pitching, he did not want to come out."

The competitive spirit in Cory Lidle was evident even in the early days of his professional career. Signed as an amateur free agent by the Minnesota Twins in 1990, his first stop en route to the major leagues was with the Twins Gulf Coast League team in 1991 where he went 1-1 in four games. He followed the next season with a 2-1 mark with Elizabethtown of the Appalachian League.

Before the start of the 1993 season, Lidle was released by the Minnesota organization and then signed with Pocatello of the Pioneer League, where he went 8-4 in 17 games. He spent the next three seasons in the Milwaukee Brewers organization with mixed results, but had his breakout season in 1996 with the New York Mets farm club in Binghampton where he went 14-10 with a fine 3.31 ERA. After a 4-2 start with Norfolk of the International League in 1997, Lidle got his first taste of major league action pitching in 54 games for the Mets with a 7-2 record.

Selected by the Arizona Diamondbacks in the expansion draft, Lidle was injured for most of the 1998 campaign and was claimed off waivers by Tampa Bay. He was 1-0 in limited action with the Devil Rays in 1999 and split the 2000 season between AAA Durham (6-2) and Tampa Bay (4-6). Following that season, Lidle was traded to Oakland where he had an impressive 13-6 record for the A's in 2001 which he followed up with an 8-10 mark the following year.

Another trade saw him packing north of the border to Toronto where he was 12-15 in 2003 before splitting the 2004 campaign between Cincinnati and Philadelphia, with a 12-12 mark. In his first full year with the Phillies, he was 13-11 in 2005 and had developed the reputation as a pitcher who took the ball every five days and usually gave his team a chance to win. In fact, he started more games with Philadelphia than any other major league team he pitched with.

But prior to the 2006 season, Cory Lidle developed a strong interest in flying.

"It was actually toward the end of 2005 that he started showing us a tutorial on his laptop computer about how to fly," said Dan Stephenson, manager of video production for the Phillies organization. "He said he was going to get his pilot's license before spring training of 2006. He was very into it and threw himself completely into learning how to fly. He just loved it. He looked at it as something he would be doing for the rest of his life.

"Cory was a real nice guy who was pretty well rounded. A good family man, he was very friendly and approachable. He wasn't what you could classify as a dumb jock. He did a lot of preparation before the game. He'd get upset if we didn't have tape of the opposition hitters who he was going to face. He wanted to see the approach that pitchers who were similar to him took against the team he was pitching against. He knew he wasn't going out there with Curt Schilling stuff. He needed to plan and he knew his limitations. Cory was not a thrower, he was a pitcher."

But when he wasn't pitching, most of his energy was dedicated to his new-found hobby, flying. After getting his pilot's license, he purchased a $187,000 single-engine, four-seat Cirrus SR20 light aircraft. He often stated how safe the plane was, in part because it had a parachute that was designed to lower the plane slowly to safety.

"I'm not worried about the flying," Lidle said in an interview. "I'm safe up there. I feel very comfortable with my abilities flying an airplane."

While those who cared about him did have concerns about the dangers that were present, the pitcher had great confidence in his piloting ability.

"You always have concerns when someone is doing something dangerous," said Dubee. "But when you talked to him about it, he'd tell you about all of the lessons he had and things like detailed flight plans. He was as determined as he could be."

Lidle spent most of the 2006 season with the Phillies, sporting an 8-7 record in 21 games. But with the team foundering, he was traded along with All Star right fielder Bobby Abreu to the New York Yankees for four prospects. New York General Manager Brian Cashman stated that he would not have made the deal had Lidle not been included. He went 4-3 for the Bronx Bombers and seemed to have a good chance to be re-signed by the team for the 2007 season.

But after the Yankees were eliminated from the playoffs by the Detroit Tigers, Lidle's wife, Melanie, and their six-year-old son Christopher boarded a commercial flight back home to the Los Angeles area. On the same day, Lidle and his flight instructor, Tyler Stanger, would begin flying his new plane to his West Covina home.

The pair took off from the nearby airport in Teterboro, N.J., at 2:30 p.m., not having any idea that their lives would suddenly and violently end less than 15 minutes later when the plane inexplicably crashed into the luxury apartment building. The cause remains a mystery. As a result of the crash, access to certain New York air space by private planes was limited by authorities.

In an article published in the *New York Times* less than a month before the deaths of Lidle and Stanger, the pitcher's flying ability was described.

"On the mound he has to hold in all the emotion and keep completely focused. It's the same with flying. If you're in an emergency, you can't waste time worrying. You have to take control of the situation. A lot of people I fly with don't have that mentality. Cory does."

Those comments were made by Lidle's flight instructor Tyler Stanger, who died with him on that gloomy October afternoon. One can only wonder what emergency caused such a tragic accident that cost two young lives.

"It was a tremendous shock," said Rich Dubee. "You would never imagine this happening."

SOMETIMES
IN WINTER

D avid Clayton Thomas and Blood, Sweat & Tears performed the haunting song, "Sometimes in Winter," in the late 1960s. There are those who live their lives by the seasons of baseball. At some point in the careers of many players, the end of a baseball season can mean the end of a career. Sometimes, the end of a season can be the last glimpse at an athlete who had unknowingly said his final goodbye.

In the gray winter that separates baseball seasons, people die without having the opportunity to experience another year of America's Pastime. Ballplayers are many things, but first and foremost, human. They are frail and mortal and subject to the same life-threatening situations as everyone else. While retirement, injuries, and the old 12-to-6 breaking ball can end careers before spring training begins, major league players can also die shockingly and suddenly in the off-season.

There are numerous examples of such untimely deaths. But occasionally, reality just seems a little much. It is often said that bad things happen in sets of three. There can be no arguing that was the case between the 1976 and 1977 baseball seasons. For it was during that off-season that three active and vibrant players were tragically killed. Adding to the irony is the fact that all three died within a three-month period.

Shortly after the end of the '76 season, Pirates pitcher Bob Moose died when his car crashed on a slippery road in Ohio at a celebration of his 29th birthday. Following a golf outing, teammates and friends waited at the gathering for the guest of honor who would never arrive.

Moose had a career filled with ups and downs, but he was also blessed with the perfect makeup for someone with such challenges. He also had the proper mind-set to be a relief pitcher. There was some thought in the Pittsburgh organization that Moose might well be groomed to eventually become the Bucs closer. Such plans, if they actually existed, were forgotten after that rainy afternoon.

Another pitcher who had seen more than his share of ups and downs during his career was Danny Frisella. Enjoying a rebirth with Milwaukee, the forkball specialist was anxiously awaiting the start of a new baseball season and the birth of a new child. There was no doubt that his life was on the upswing. He was so psyched about spring training and a new child that he and his wife spent the winter in Phoenix, close to the Brewers training facility. That was a tragic decision.

After a bright start with the New York Mets, injuries saddled Frisella. But after a number of stops along the way, he appeared to have found a home with the Brewers, who appreciated his experience and guile on the pitcher's mound. And no matter where Danny Frisella played, his friendly, outgoing personality made him a favorite among his teammates.

But a seemingly innocent dune buggy ride on New Year's Day ended in tragedy for the pitcher who would never complete his come-back or meet his new son.

Less than a week after Frisella's death, young Mike Miley died in an automobile accident near his beloved Louisiana State University, where he starred in baseball and football. A top draft pick with the

California Angels, he was being groomed to play shortstop for the next decade or so. Rather than lose their young star of the future to free agency, the Angels agreed to give him increased playing time in the major leagues. His first two trials in the major leagues were brief and no doubt frustrating. But with increased playing time and more experience, it appeared that stardom was just around the corner for this former All-American baseball star at LSU.

For fans of these three fine players, it was in the words of the Blood, Sweat & Tears song, "The spring of frozen rain."

#38

BOB MOOSE

Courtesy of the Pittsburgh Pirates.

Pittsburgh Pirates
Pitcher

Bats: Right; Throws: Right
Height: 6 ft.; Weight: 200 lbs.

Born: October 9, 1947, in Export, Pa.
Died: October 9, 1976, in Martins Ferry, Ohio

Drafted by the Pirates in the 18th round of the 1965 amateur
  draft.
10 Seasons   76 Wins   71 Losses

DIED ON HIS BIRTHDAY

In the mid-1970s, the Pittsburgh Pirates enjoyed quite a string of successful seasons including their World Championship 1971 campaign. The following year, the defending champions advanced to the postseason for the third consecutive year to take on the Cincinnati Reds. The winner of that National League Championship Series would then move on to the Fall Classic.

Both teams were deadlocked at two wins apiece for a decisive Game Five to be held in Cincinnati. The Pirates had a 3-2 advantage until Johnny Bench hit a solo home run to tie things up in the ninth inning. In what was to be Hall of Fame outfielder Roberto Clemente's final baseball game, the Reds advanced to the World Series when Pirates reliever Bob Moose uncorked a wild pitch that allowed George Foster to score the winning run from third base. While the Reds went to the World Series, the Pirates simply went home.

Being the person who threw the wild pitch that ousted his team from the playoffs could literally destroy a pitcher. But Bob Moose was a guy who believed in himself and had a great mind-set for a ballplayer.

"He just dealt with it," said pitcher Steve Blass, who won 19 games for the 1972 Pirates. "He shrugged it off. Bob had a wonderful positive attitude. He was a great guy with the ideal temperament for a ballplayer. He had a great approach to what he did, was a fine guy and an ideal teammate."

Nearly four years later, on October 9, 1976, Moose was killed on his 29th birthday in a two-car accident in Martins Ferry, Ohio. He was on his way to a party being held after a golf outing organized by former Pirate Bill Mazeroski.

"I was out of baseball at the time," said Blass. "I was at a seminar and heard about it and was in shock. We had been teammates. It was just so sudden. A wild pitch can be abrupt, but nothing compared to real life."

Another former teammate of Moose's, pitcher Jim Rooker, was at the restaurant waiting for his friend to arrive.

"The hardest part was waiting at the restaurant for him," Rooker recalled. "Bob and I drove down together to play in the event. It turned into a rainy night. He was on his way when he had the accident. We were waiting when a couple of cops came and starting talking to Mazeroski at the door. I looked at his face and you just knew something serious had happened.

"From the police report, he hit the shoulder of the road and veered back and the car hydroplaned and hit another oncoming car. There was no alcohol, no speeding. Just bad, stupid luck and bad weather."

Moose's life with the Pirates organization began when he was drafted by the team in the 18th round of the 1965 amateur draft. Right out of the box, he showed promise beyond his draft credentials while pitching for Salem of the Appalachian League that very summer. Moose led the league in winning percentage with an 8-2 record with a 1.95 ERA.

The following season, he continued to open the eyes of the Pirates organization with a combined 11-5 record split between Gastonia (N.C.) and Raleigh with 122 strikeouts in 138 innings. In 1967, his second full season as a professional, he went 6-2 with Macon of the Southern League and 4-1 with Columbus of the International League, earning him a late-season call-up to Pittsburgh where he earned his first big league win in two appearances. Bob Moose was a major league pitcher.

"Our first encounter was in Triple A when I was pitching for Toledo and he was pitching for Columbus in the Governor's Cup Championship Game," said Rooker. "I happened to beat him in that game, 1-0. He gave up two hits in the game and I gave up one. I didn't know him, but after the game I took a bottle of champagne to their locker room and gave it to him. When I became a Pirate in '73 he remembered that and we became instant friends.

"We both liked fishing and had other interests in common. We became good, close friends, real buddies. As a player, what I remember in terms of ability was his unhittable slider. He was a great guy to be around, a real competitor and bulldog type of guy. Bob was an incredible competitor who had a great attitude. Nothing mattered to him, nothing bothered him. He'd just say, 'I don't care.'"

The right-hander had a good major league fastball, but his out pitch was a slider that could give opposing batters fits.

"He had a great slider," said Steve Blass. "I remember he used to torment Richie Allen of the Philadelphia Phillies with it. They used to have some great battles. He would either strike him out or Allen would hit a smash somewhere."

As a 20-year-old in 1968, Moose was a spot starter and reliever in Pittsburgh going 8-12 with a fine 2.74 ERA. He pitched well beyond his experience and exhibited an excellent strikeout-to-walk ratio, one of the key ingredients to being a successful major league hurler.

The following year, he became a dominating pitcher, leading the National League with a winning percentage of .824 en route to a 14-3 record. He fanned 165 batters in 170 innings and earned a spot in baseball immortality on September 20 when he threw a no-hitter against the New York Mets. In the 170 innings, he yielded just nine home runs to opposing batters.

While Moose had all of the tools necessary to succeed in the major leagues, he also had the perfect makeup for a pitcher. He was a happy-go-lucky individual off the playing field and a ballplayer who was full of self confidence on the field.

"He had complete confidence in himself," commented Blass, "one of the best outlooks as a ballplayer I've seen, like a tunnel vision. He was not going to fail. And he was a great guy, as good a friend and solid a teammate as you could have. He was uninhibited, gregarious, and a free spirit. The kind of guy who really lightened up the clubhouse."

Primarily a starter, Moose was a steady double-digit winner for the Pirates who could throw strikes and was very stingy surrendering home runs to opposing batters.

He was sidelined for most of the season in 1974 because of a blood clot in his right armpit. He pitched in just seven games that year with a 1-5 record. Following the season, he underwent a rare operation in which one of his ribs was removed in order to free the blood clot.

The following season he spent time pitching with Charleston of the International League before coming back to Pittsburgh. He had a 2-2 record for the Pirates in 23 games, but more important, Moose served notice that he was once again healthy enough to help the pitching staff.

He came back strong in 1976, pitching in 53 games, all but two out of the bullpen, with a 3-9 record. Still young at the age of 28, it was widely assumed that Moose was being groomed to be the Pirates next closer.

"He had the ability and the stuff," said Jim Rooker. "One of the reasons he went down hill was an injury he received on his pitching thumb. Until it healed, he could not get the proper grip on his slider or fastball. Once it healed, he re-grouped and starting getting it back together.

"When he started to struggle they sent him to the bullpen. A lot of guys can't handle that sort of thing. He just accepted things without question. Openly, he didn't make waves when he was sent to the pen. His demeanor never changed."

But, unfortunately, on his 29th birthday on the way to a party, police stated that in a light rain, Moose's car went onto the bank of a busy road and swerved back, colliding with another vehicle head-on. The driver and passenger from the other car were released from a local hospital. Two women passengers in Moose's car were injured.

"There is no telling what he could have done because he was such a strong guy," said Rooker. "He didn't look like a pitcher, he looked like a guard on the football field. He could have had a 15- or 18-year career. A lot of your success depends on the team, but he would have done his part.

"I still think of him all the time. I think of how crazy he was and what a maniac he was. When I think of him, it's not a sad thing because he didn't live a sad life."

DANNY FRISELLA

Danny with his wife Pam.
Courtesy of Pam Frisella.

Milwaukee Brewers
Pitcher

Bats: Left; Throws: Right
Height: 6 ft.;
    Weight: 195 lbs.

Born: March 4, 1946,
    in San Francisco, Calif.
Died: January 1, 1977,
    in Phoenix, Ariz.

Acquired by the Milwaukee Brewers from the St. Louis
    Cardinals on June 7, 1976, for a player to be named later
    (Sam Mejias).

10 Seasons   34 Wins   40 Losses   57 Saves   3.32 ERA

RELIEVER LIVED LIFE
TO THE FULLEST

By the time he reached his 30th birthday, Danny Frisella had pretty
much done it all in baseball. A third-round draft choice by the New
York Mets in the amateur draft of 1966, he pitched his first major

league game the following season. He even pitched briefly for the World Championship team of 1969.

A successful starter in the minor leagues, Frisella achieved most of his success out of the bullpen in the majors. Coming up to a Mets team that had starters such as Tom Seaver, Nolan Ryan, Gary Gentry, and Jim McAndrew, Frisella's making a name for himself pitching out of the bullpen was as good as it would get.

After spending his first six seasons with the Mets, Frisella became a bit of a journeyman, overcoming arm and shoulder problems to once again pitch extremely well for the Milwaukee Brewers in 1976.

While he had done much in the game by the time he reached his 30th birthday, tragically, Danny Frisella would never reach his 31st birthday. He was killed on New Year's Day 1977 in a dune buggy accident on a country road outside of Phoenix. He and another man apparently lost control of the vehicle, which flipped over.

Not experienced in such vehicles, Frisella attempted to jump out of the dune buggy, only to have his foot get caught. He was killed when the dune buggy landed on top of him. If he had remained in the vehicle, he almost certainly not only would have survived, but may not have even sustained any injuries.

The promise of a fun New Year's dinner with family, friends, and football soon turned into a day of tears. He and his wife, Pam, had a son, Jason, who was three-and-a-half at the time. They were expecting another child at the time of Frisella's death.

"The Brewers were going to have spring training in Phoenix and since I was pregnant we decided to move out there early and get settled," said Pam Frisella. "It was New Year's Day and Danny and a friend of ours went for a ride on the dune buggy. The last thing he said was that he'd be home for the Rose Bowl. My parents had come out from Detroit for New Year's Eve so my father was there to catch me when I found out."

Two months after Danny Frisella's death, Pam gave birth to their second son, Daniel Jr., who was born on March 4, 1977, ironically, his father's birthday.

Danny Frisella was the same fun-loving person at the ballpark and away from baseball.

"If I were to describe Danny the word I'd use is 'casual,'" said Pam Frisella. "I don't think I ever saw Danny hurry. Our son Daniel is the same way. They just know that life is the way it is and you're not going to change it. Danny had the ability to draw people to him. He was just so much fun to be around. That's probably why I never remarried.

"He was one of the last players that would have paid them to play. He just loved to play baseball. He loved the excitement and the challenge. And he had a devil-may-care attitude. He just understood that winning and losing can change daily. If you win today don't get too excited because you could very well lose tomorrow."

After signing his first professional contract with the Mets, Frisella was sent to Class A Auburn of the NY-PA league. In 10 games, he had a 5-4 record with an impressive 2.96 ERA. The following season, 1967, Frisella was a rising star in the Mets minor league system, starting out with a 9-3 record with Durham of the Carolina League. He was overpowering, allowing just 83 hits in 109 innings pitched, while striking out 121 and walking just 23.

His hot start earned him a promotion to AAA Jacksonville of the International League where the right-hander continued to impress with a 2-2 record in eight games with a 3.09 ERA. The Mets then brought him up to the parent club where he struggled in 14 games, winning only one of seven decisions. But his ERA was a solid 3.41 showing that he was certainly capable of competing on the major league level.

During the next two seasons, Frisella split time between the Mets and more minor league time learning his craft. In 1968, he was 2-4 in New York, earning his first two big league saves. The following season, he appeared in just three contests with the Mets after going 11-2 for Triple A Tidewater.

But while playing winter ball following the season, Danny Frisella learned how to throw a specialty pitch that would help make him an effective pitcher for the rest of his career. Veteran pitcher Diego Segui taught him the forkball.

In 1970, armed with his new weapon, he started out with a 7-3 record in 13 games with Tidewater. Frisella made the majors to stay, pitching well in 30 games, garnering an 8-3 record with an impressive 3.02 ERA. The next year he spent the entire season with the Mets with a 5-8 record and 9 saves.

After the conclusion of the 1972 season, he was traded to the Atlanta Braves along with pitcher Gary Gentry in exchange for George Stone and Felix Millan.

Frisella spent two seasons with the Braves with a combined record of 4-6 with 14 saves, pitching for a team that had not yet become the powerhouse that fans have become so familiar with. While he was pitching with the Braves, Danny and Pam Frisella met another baseball couple with whom they became very close friends, Phil and Nancy Niekro. The wives began a friendship that the husbands soon enjoyed as well.

"Well I knew of Danny, of course, when he was pitching against us with the Mets," Phil Niekro, a winner of 318 major league games and a member of the Baseball Hall of Fame said. "We didn't know each other except to say hello to on the field. But then when he came to the Braves, our wives became really good friends. The Braves had a very active wives club and they did a lot of things together. Those two really hit it off and then we became great friends too. Usually it takes a long time for good friendships to take place, sometimes years. But it was amazing how close we became as friends. With Danny and Pam and Nancy and me, it was an instant friendship. We all just had a good comfort level with each other."

A competitor on the field, Frisella was a very popular player in the clubhouse. His teammates knew he was giving it everything he had on the playing field and respected the person, not just the pitcher.

"He was a very competitive guy," noted Niekro. "He was always funny, laughing, telling a good joke. I never really saw him get really mad, or upset. He really taught me something. His attitude was that it's not where you've been, it's where you're going. We have no control over yesterday and tomorrow may never come. The only thing we can control is now.

"He was just one of the guys who liked everybody and everybody liked him. He knew it was a team and it took all 25 guys to win. Every job was as important as someone else's. When he went out to the mound, it was just as important as Hank Aaron coming up with the bases loaded."

Following the 1974 season, Frisella was sent to the San Diego Padres in exchange for power-hitting outfielder, Cito Gaston.

Mired with another poor team in San Diego, Frisella had a 1-6 record, but was a workhorse pitching in a career high 65 games with a 3.13 ERA and 9 saves. His stellar work caught the eye of the St. Louis Cardinals organization, which sent pitcher Ken Reynolds along with Bob Stewart to the Padres in exchange for Frisella. He pitched well for the Cardinals in 18 games, but was then traded to Milwaukee on June 7, 1976, for a player to be named later, who turned out to be Sam Mejias.

Frisella and Milwaukee seemed to be made for each other. The veteran hurler sported a 5-2 record with 9 saves and a 2.74 ERA in 32 games for the Brewers. His experience and guile on the mound, along with an outstanding forkball would have made him a key element on the Milwaukee staff in 1977.

But then the tragic accident on New Year's Day ended the story. Sadly, he and his wife, Pam, never had the chance to enjoy their post-baseball dream of living in La Jolla, Calif., and opening a jewelry store. He never lived to see Danny Jr. or brighten up the lives of those around him again.

"My wife heard about it and called upstairs to ask if I had heard about what happened to Danny," remembered Phil Niekro. "If he had stayed in the dune buggy he would have been okay. When I heard about it, I think I just sat down and cried."

MIKE
MILEY

Courtesy of Angels Baseball.

California Angels
Shortstop

Bats: Both; Throws: Right
Height: 6 ft. 1 in.;
   Weight: 185 lbs.

Born: March 30, 1953,
   in Yazoo City, Miss.
Died: January 6, 1977, in Baton Rouge, La.

Drafted in the first round of the 1974 amateur draft by the
   California Angels.
2 Seasons   .176 BA   4 HR   30 RBIs   1 SB

GIFTED ATHLETE KILLED
IN AUTOMOBILE ACCIDENT

To the average sport fan, the name Mike Miley might bring back
memories of the 1974 Orange Bowl. Miley quarterbacked the
Louisiana State University Tigers to the Bowl appearance against
undefeated Penn State. Although the Nittany Lions won the context
by a 16-9 score, the Tigers beat three undefeated teams en route to

Miami that season. A four-sport letterman, Miley is considered by many to be the greatest athlete in LSU history.

Baseball was his first love. The lanky shortstop was drafted in the first round of the 1971 amateur draft by the Cincinnati Reds, but did not sign, preferring to attend college. Then, when the California Angels made him the 10th pick in the first round of the 1974 draft, he signed on the dotted line, passing up his senior year at LSU, to sign with the Angels.

His high pedigree in the draft is no real surprise considering the kinds of numbers he put up at LSU. In 1972 he hit .333 with eight homers and 31 RBIs. The following year, he hit the ball at a .273 clip. In his senior season of 1974, Miley's all-around ability earned him First Team, All-American status with a .275 average.

Miley was assigned to Double A El Paso of the Texas League where he hit a solid .288 with 13 homers and 45 RBIs that season. In 1975, he started out the season at Triple A Salt Lake City where he hit just .209, but was recalled to the Angels where he hit .179 in his first 70 major league games with four homers and 26 RBIs. The parent club was struggling and this was a good time to take a look at less experienced players who might have a bright major league future.

"As such a high draft pick, he was rushed along and maybe got a chance to play at the major league level before he was ready," said Jerry Remy, a 10-year big league veteran who spent three years with the Angels and was a teammate of Miley's. "In those days, we were not a very good team. That's how I made it. Some guys play four or five years in the minors to get ready.

"He was a great athlete. I always think of him as being a real quiet guy with that southern accent. He played shortstop and I played second base. So we played next to each other, but I'm not sure for how many games."

Needing more seasoning and experience, the top draft pick played most of the 1976 season with Salt Lake City and responded with his best pro season, letting it be known that he was knocking on the major league door. Miley hit .274 in 119 games with six home runs, 60 RBIs, and 28 stolen bases.

He appeared in 14 games with the Angels that year, hitting just .184. But his solid season at Triple A Salt Lake City gave hope that he was ready to be an everyday player in the major leagues. Being able to play on the major league level is not an easy accomplishment, no matter how much raw ability is there. On-the-job training in the big leagues can be difficult.

"That's tough in any job," said Jerry Remy. "You have the ability and the talent, but it's tough to adjust in the major leagues. Once they find out what you can't do, they expose it and you have to adjust. It's not an easy place to learn because there is such a high level of competition."

Miley toyed with the idea of free agency that winter, but he chose to re-sign with the Angels when he was assured that he would have a spot on the California roster, probably as a back-up to Bobby Grich. The on-the-job training and his solid minor league credentials had the Angels feeling confident that Miley would soon be ready to assume everyday status with the Angels, if not in 1977, in the very near future.

But that dream ended on January 6, 1977, when Miley was killed in a one-car accident in Baton Rouge. His sports car ran off a curve and crashed into a culvert. He was thrown from the car, which then rolled over on him, causing fatal injuries.

Authorities said he was driving at a high rate of speed.

···

PLAYERS WHO DIED IN AUTOMOBILE ACCIDENTS

···

A short ride down most any highway usually includes a makeshift memorial on the side of the road where a person's life was lost in an automobile accident. The arrangement of flowers, pictures, stuffed animals, and other personal mementos give grieving friends and relatives an opportunity for some measure of closure and also acts as a warning to drivers passing by.

There are about 6.4 million automobile accidents every year resulting in approximately 3 million injuries, 2 million permanent injuries, and 40,000 deaths annually in the United States. Department of Transportation statistics indicate that most accidents are generally caused by poor driving behavior.

Forty percent of fatalities are related to drinking and driving, 30 percent are due to speeding, and the remainder of fatal crashes occurs when a vehicle goes off the road. In spite of these shocking statistics and a national media campaign that has lasted decades, only 68 percent of drivers wear seat belts nationwide even though it saves lives and prevents serious injury.

Automobile accidents remain the top killer of people in the United States up to the age of 37. When a baseball player begins to make some money, one of the first things he is apt to purchase is a new car. And more often than not, the vehicle is a racy, fast, powerful machine that offers far more horsepower than is safe for the average driver.

Just because a person has outstanding ability on a baseball field does not ensure he'll be able to handle a lean, mean, racing machine that so many of them buy.

The list of baseball players killed in automobile accidents is alarming, although probably not above the national average. But the number of sad stories and broken dreams are heartbreaking with professional athletes, just as they are with those who live their lives out of the spotlight.

Mike Sharperson had clawed his way back to the pinnacle of his career, being recalled from the minor leagues to play with the San Diego Padres. But he never arrived home that night to pack.

Mike Darr, by all accounts, was not only a fine young outfielder with the Padres, but a good guy and a solid family man as well. But his life ended prematurely when he and some friends were involved in a frightening crash after a night out.

Paul Edmondson had shown some promise as a spot starter with the Chicago White Sox in 1969. But his career and life went up in smoke in a fiery crash in California. Veteran infielder Chico Ruiz had just become a U.S. citizen and was looking forward to earning a roster spot with the Kansas City Royals. But he lost his life in a crash before going to spring training.

In some of these instances and others, the fault lies with the driver who may have been drinking, or driving with excessive speed. Or, the fatal accident was just that, an accident, with no one to blame. But regardless of who was to blame in a particular fatal accident, it's fair to wonder how many would have survived if they had simply buckled up.

WOODY CROWSON

Philadelphia Athletics
Pitcher

Bats: Right; Throws: Right
Height: 6 ft. 2 in.; Weight: 185 lbs.

Born: September 9, 1918, in Fuquay Springs, N.C.
Died: August 14, 1947, in Mayodan, N.C.

1 Season   0 Wins   0 Losses   6.00 ERA

KILLED IN CRASH WITH
FORMER BIG LEAGUE PITCHER

Like many players of his era, Thomas Woodrow "Woody" Crowson traveled a long way for a short period of time in the major leagues. The native of Fuquay Springs, N.C., was with the Philadelphia Athletics during the early stages of the 1945 baseball season. The 26-year-old pitched in just one major league game.

On April 17 of that year, he made his big league appearance, which lasted three innings. In his stint, he surrendered two earned runs on two hits, gave up two walks, but also struck out a pair. Not a bad outing, particularly considering that it was his big league debut.

One game, no decision, 6.00 ERA. And with that, the major league baseball career of Woody Crowson was over. Competition for roster spots was incredibly tough in those days and many pitchers with major league ability spent years riding buses in the minors looking for another chance.

That's just what this tall right-hander was doing, riding buses, playing the game he loved and hoping for another chance to play in the major leagues. Two years later, he was pitching with the Greensboro team of the Carolina League, still trying to open some eyes and get another shot at The Show. But fate was not a friend of Woody Crowson.

On August 14, 1947, Crowson and the rest of his Greensboro teammates were riding the team bus in Mayodan, N.C., going from one series to another. It was a typical day, typical of the minor leagues. But then the quiet bus ride suddenly changed and Woody Crowson was the unluckiest person on the team bus.

The bus carrying the Greensboro team was involved in an accident with a truck loaded with watermelons. The only fatality of the incident was Woody Crowson. His big league dreams, and his life, were suddenly over.

Adding a weird sort of irony to the tragic story is that the driver of the watermelon truck was none other that a 14-year major league veteran, former pitcher Van Lingle Mungo.

A weird story. A tragic death.

A potential never fulfilled.

JAY DAHL

....

Houston Astros
Pitcher

Bats: Both; Throws: Left
Height: 5 ft. 10 in.; Weight: 183 lbs.

Born: December 5, 1945, in San Bernardino, Calif.
Died: June 20, 1965, in Salisbury, N.C.

Signed as an amateur free agent by the Houston Colt .45s prior
   to the 1963 season.
1 Season   0 Wins   1 Loss   16.88 ERA

THE YOUNGEST FORMER
MAJOR LEAGUE PLAYER TO DIE

When 17-year-old rookie left-hander Jay Dahl started for the
Houston Colt .45s against the New York Mets on September 27,
1963, he became part of major league history. He was the starting
pitcher in an all-rookie lineup employed by Houston, the first all-
rookie lineup in the history of the game.

Although his debut was far from successful as he gave up seven
runs in three innings en route to his first and last loss in the big
leagues, being in the majors was quite an accomplishment, particularly for such a young prospect. Who would have thought that less
than two years later, Dahl would once again be part of major league
history by becoming the youngest former major league player to die?

While pitching for Salisbury of the Western Carolinas League, Dahl pitched his team into first place by beating Gastonia (N.C.), 7-3, on June 19. That evening, the Astros players were the guests of a dinner at the home of G. M. Hamilton, the Salisbury club president. Dahl and Gary Marshall, a 19-year-old pitcher on the team, left to attend a movie with Patricia Ann Troutman, a 20-year-old secretary.

As the ballplayers were returning Troutman to her home, the auto, which is believed to have been driven by Marshall, was traveling at a high rate of speed when it hit a patch of sand on a Salisbury street and went out of control, hitting a tree. Troutman was killed instantly.

Jay Dahl died of internal injuries hours after the accident at Rowan Memorial Hospital. Marshall, a native of Hutchinson, Kans., was taken to a hospital in Winston-Salem. He suffered a broken right arm and broken right leg, and his injuries also forced the removal of his left eye. The vision in his right eye was lost as it was damaged beyond repair.

A North Carolina prisoner offered one of his eyes in a transplant to Marshall in the hope he would be able to see again. But doctors felt the transplant would not result in Marshall regaining his vision.

While Dahl was not pitching in the major leagues at the time of his death, he seemed to be on a fast track back to the majors as his 5-0 record with Salisbury would indicate.

For trivia buffs, the all-rookie lineup of September 27, 1963, included a number of players who had long major league careers. The starters that day were pitcher Jay Dahl (17 years old), catcher Jerry Grote (19 years old), first baseman Rusty Staub (19 years old), second baseman Joe Morgan (20 years old), third baseman Glenn Vaughan (19 years old), shortstop Roland "Sonny" Jackson (19 years old), and outfielders Brock Davis (19 years old), Aaron Pointer (21 years old), and Jimmy Wynn (21 years old).

Additionally, two other left-handed pitchers made their major league debuts in relief of Dahl that day, Joe Hoerner and Danny Coombs.

MIKE DARR

Mike Darr, right, with life-long friend Darrin Chiaverini, center, and sportscaster Ryan Chiaverini, left.

Courtesy of Darrin Chiaverini.

San Diego Padres
Outfield

Bats: Left; Throws: Right
Height: 6 ft. 3 in.; Weight: 205 lbs.

Born: March 21, 1976, in Corona, Calif.
Died: February 15, 2002, in Phoenix, Ariz.

Acquired by the San Diego Padres from the Detroit Tigers
with Matt Skrmetta for Jody Reed on March 22, 1997.

3 Seasons   .273 BA   5 HR   67 RBIs

TOP YOUNG OUTFIELD
PROSPECT KILLED IN CRASH

When Mike Darr and Darrin Chiaverini were growing up in Corona,
Calif., they were not all that different from typical kids who dreamed
of what life held in store for them. Both were exceptional athletes.
But for two kids from a quiet California town to grow up to be a professional baseball and a professional football player is amazing stuff.

While the pair of good friends didn't dwell on their dreams for
the future, they did discuss the irony of just how far each had come
after their professional careers had begun.

"We were best friends," Austin Wranglers wide receiver Darrin
Chiaverini said about his childhood friend, Mike Darr. "He was my
high school quarterback. We grew up playing baseball and football
together as kids. We were friends since we were 10 or 11. He grew
up and played pro baseball and I play pro football.

"At the time, we just enjoyed being kids and playing sports. As
kids you dream about the pros, but you don't know if it will ever happen. But after the fact, we were both just sitting around the house in
Corona and I was with the Dallas Cowboys and he was with the
Padres. How could two childhood friends from the same little town
grow up to be professional athletes? His two kids were playing with
my two kids. There we were, professional athletes who grew up
together watching my two kids and his two kids playing together
wondering what the future held for them.

"At the time I didn't know how little time he had left. Mike was
a great guy. I really miss him. He was different, the kind of guy who

kept to himself. But once you got to know him you found out what a great guy he was. I consider him my best friend."

When Mike Darr came up to the San Diego Padres in 1999, he had all the credentials of a player destined to have a long, successful career. After being acquired by San Diego in March 1997 from the Detroit Tigers organization, all the hard hitter from the left side of the plate did was hit .344 for Rancho Cucamonga in the California League, good enough to become Padres Minor League Player of the Year.

A solid .310 follow-up season with Mobile of the Southern League set Darr up for the 1999 campaign, which he started with the Las Vegas AAA farm club. After 100 games and a solid .298 batting average, he was recalled by the parent club and hit big league pitching at a .271 clip in 25 games.

After splitting the 2000 season between Las Vegas (.344 average, splitting Minor League Player of the Year honors once again with Jeremy Owens) and San Diego (.268 average), Darr saw plenty of action for the Padres in 2001. The 25-year-old played in a career high 105 games in which he hit an impressive .277. Unlike many players who have trouble with pitchers who throw from their side of the plate, Darr hit well against left-handed pitchers. The sky seemed the limit for this outfielder with a strong arm, good speed, and great attitude.

"I don't think he ever reached his potential," commented Chiaverini. "When he was young, he was a beast on the playing field. He was a real five-tool player who could hit, hit for power, throw, field, and run. Michael wasn't into steroids or anything. He did it all on his natural ability. With all of the ability he had, I think he would have developed into a 25 to 30 home run guy. He was nowhere near his potential."

But as pitchers and catchers gathered in Phoenix for the 2002 spring training, tragedy struck. Darr and another childhood friend, Duane Johnson, were killed in a one-car crash on February 15. His teammate, pitcher Ben Howard, was the only person in the SUV wearing a seat belt, and he survived the accident with minor cuts and bruises. He has since pitched in the major leagues with the Padres and Florida and is currently pitching in Triple A. But there was no such future for Darr and no second chance related to drinking and driving.

The three friends' vehicle drifted into a center dirt median on the road and rolled across three lanes, crashing through a fence. Darr was just a month shy of his 26th birthday. He left behind his wife, Natalie, and two children, Mike Jr. and Matthew. Johnson was 23 years old.

Whenever drinking and driving is mentioned with a fatal automobile accident, many jump to conclusions. While there can be no justification for driving while under the influence, each case is different. Regardless of the circumstances, in cases such as this one, there were no second chances.

"What happened, happened," said Chiaverini. "You wish you could change it but we've all driven when we shouldn't have. He was taking pain killers because he was having some problems with his shoulder and probably had a couple of beers. Michael wasn't a big drinker. I think the mix caused him to fall asleep behind the wheel, rather than just crashing. Unfortunately fate doesn't give you a second chance.

"My dad called me at five in the morning on the day it happened and was screaming on the phone that Mike had died. I spoke with him the day before. He was going to take some batting practice and call me that night. He never did.

"I was just blown away. I called the house and went over to be with the family since I lived about five minutes away. It was surreal. His oldest son was there and his wife Natalie was crying.

"He was a great person and everybody makes mistakes. I just hope that everyone will judge themselves before they judge anyone else. I really miss him. It was very hard for me and I had a tough couple of years. Our friend Duane Johnson and Michael were in my backyard one day and Duane's uncle, Gary Scott, was telling Michael to slow down. He had a real carefree attitude. Who doesn't at 24, or

25? That keeps coming back to me because two months later, he got killed."

Darr played baseball, basketball, and football at Corona High School. His dad, Mike, played briefly for the Toronto Blue Jays.

He was a second-round draft choice of the Detroit Tigers in 1994 and was known to have the strongest throwing arm in the San Diego system after he was acquired in a trade in 1997. While he did not hit for power, he was a line drive hitter who had the speed to take an extra base.

His solid 2001 season in which he played all three outfield positions made him a cinch to be a regular with the Padres in 2002 due to the retirement of Tony Gwynn and the opening created when Ricky Henderson left the team as a free agent. Darr was even pictured on the 2002 media guide of the Padres and was looked to be a bright spot for years to come in the San Diego outfield.

JOE DESA

....

Chicago White Sox
First Base/Outfield

Bats: Left; Throws: Left
Height: 5 ft. 11 in.; Weight: 170 lbs.

Born: July 27, 1959, in Honolulu, Hawaii
Died: December 20, 1986, in San Juan, Puerto Rico

Signed as a free agent by the Kansas City Royals on
   November 15, 1986.
2 Seasons   .200 BA   2 HR   7 RBIs

A FRESH START STOPPED
BY A TRAGIC ACCIDENT

Joe DeSa was one of those players who would never go away. He was always right on the cusp of major league baseball. A fine minor league hitter, after two cups of coffee in the majors five years apart, DeSa signed a free agent contract with the Kansas City Royals in November 1986 with the hope of being a left-handed bat off the bench and a guy who played first base and the outfield.

But that December as DeSa was playing for the first place Ponce Lions, he was killed in a two-car crash on Puerto Rico's main cross island expressway just five days before Christmas. Both cars involved in the head-on collision had no other passengers involved, and the driver of the other automobile was also killed.

DeSa and his teammates had defeated the Mayaguez Indians, 11-8, to strengthen their stranglehold on first place. DeSa was returning home to San Juan from a party at the house of one of his teammates. He was hitting .259 for the Lions at the time of the fatal crash.

A native of Honolulu, Joe DeSa was drafted by the St. Louis Cardinals in the third round of the amateur draft in 1977. The 18-year-old was sent to Calgary of the Rookie League where he had a fine inaugural season, hitting .272 with three home runs and 55 RBIs in 70 games.

In 1978, he had another fine season with St. Petersburg of the Florida State League with a .310 batting average with five homers and 30 RBIs. That production earned him a mid-season promotion to Gastonia in the Western Carolina league where he hit .262 in 42 games.

Joe DeSa came of age as a 20-year-old with AA Arkansas of the Texas League in 1979. In 130 games, he hit a solid .317 with a career high 13 home runs and 86 RBIs. The young slugger was now on the radar screen of the St. Louis Cardinals as he prepared for his first season in Triple A.

He continued his productive ways at Springfield of the American Association, hitting .293 with nine home runs and 74 RBIs in 123 games. A late-season call-up by the Cardinals saw him hit .273 in seven games.

Returning to AAA Springfield in 1981, he put together another outstanding season, hitting .292 with 12 dingers and 73 RBIs in 132 games. But there was no late-season promotion and suddenly DeSa's career seemed to be on hold.

At the end of the 1983 season, DeSa signed as a free agent with the Chicago White Sox hoping that there might be a spot for him with the Pale Hose. He got the call toward the end of the 1985 season, hitting just .182 in 28 games, although he did hit a pair of home runs and drove in seven.

In 1986, DeSa had another fine minor league campaign with Buffalo of the American Association. He played in 130 games hitting a solid .284 with 17 home runs and 83 RBIs. It was following that season, in mid-November that he signed for a new beginning with the Royals.

But sadly, five weeks later, he was killed in the two-car wreck.

PAUL EDMONDSON

Chicago White Sox
Pitcher

Bats: Right; Throws: Right
Height: 6 ft. 5 in.; Weight: 195 lbs.

Born: February 12, 1943, in Kansas City, Kans.
Died: February 13, 1970, in Santa Barbara, Calif.

Drafted in the 21st round of the 1965 amateur draft by the
Chicago White Sox.
1 Season   1 Win   6 Losses   3.70 ERA

GLIMPSES OF BIG LEAGUE TALENT

On a Chicago White Sox team that was looking for pitching, the promotion of big, right-hander Paul Edmondson to the squad in 1969 was hoped to be the shot in the arm that the Sox pitching staff was looking for. After a 7-3 start for AAA Columbus, Edmondson got his chance to pitch in The Show, with mixed reviews. The California State University graduate with a degree in business administration pitched in 14 games for Chicago. While his ERA was an acceptable 3.70, he struggled with his control, which may have been one of the major reasons for his 1-6 record.

Based on his first big league start on June 20, 1969, the White Sox confidence in him seemed totally justified as Edmondson pitched a two-hit complete game, besting the California Angels, 9-1. It proved, however, to be his lone major league victory.

After the 1-6 rookie year, Edmondson was being counted on to make a serious run at one of the starting spots in the ChiSox rotation. He had started 13 games upon his recall from Columbus and showed promise.

But the career and life of Paul Edmondson ended the day after his 27th birthday on February 13, 1970, on rain-slicked U.S. Highway Route 101. He and 22-year-old Cal Poly student Lorraine Leas were burned beyond recognition as the car he was driving, returning from a trip to San Luis Obispo, skidded out of control, crossed into the northbound lane, and sideswiped another vehicle before flipping over and bursting into flames.

The occupants of the other vehicle were not injured.

Edmondson was an outstanding athlete in college, where he starred in both baseball and basketball. On the hardwood floor, he was the leading scorer. He was an All-Conference player on the baseball squad. In his senior year, Edmondson was named San Fernando Athlete of the Year.

Paul Edmondson's early career was interrupted by military service. After breaking in with Clinton of the Midwest League in 1965, he missed most of the following season fulfilling his military obligation. Back to being a full-time baseball player in 1967, he had an 11-11 season while pitching for Lynchburg of the Carolina League.

The 1968 season saw him split time between Evansville of the Southern League and Hawaii of the Pacific Coast League with a less-than-daunting 5-14 record. But he knew how to pitch and impressed the White Sox brass with his makeup on the pitcher's mound.

His 7-3 start to the 1969 season in Columbus earned him a trip to the major leagues that, like his life, ended much too quickly.

MIKE SHARPERSON

Courtesy of the Los Angeles Dodgers.

Los Angeles Dodgers,
   Atlanta Braves
Infield

Bats: Right; Throws: Right
Height: 6 ft. 3in.;
   Weight: 191 lbs.

Born: October 4, 1961, in Orangeburg, S.C.
Died: May 26, 1996, in Las Vegas, Nev.

Signed as a free agent by the San Diego Padres in November of
   1995.
8 Seasons   .280 BA   10 HR   123 RBIs

CRASH ENDS COMEBACK DREAM

Much like many other youngsters who loved baseball, Mike
Sharperson and Herm Winningham spent countless hours playing
ball and dreaming major league dreams throughout their childhoods.
While the odds are against anyone reaching the big leagues, they had
to be astronomically against two childhood pals from the tiny town
of Orangeburg, S.C.

But the odds didn't put an end to their dreams.

"We lived down the street from each other," said Winningham. "We met when we were about seven years old and played against each other in Little League. Then we were teammates at Orangeburg-Wilkinson High School and DeKalb Junior College. We were like typical buddies growing up, playing sports together and riding our bikes all over town. We talked about playing pro baseball, hoping that some day we might get the opportunity to be in the major leagues."

Regardless of the odds, they both saw their major league dreams come true. Winningham was drafted in the first round of the 1981 Amateur Draft by the New York Mets. He went on to play nine seasons in The Show with New York, Montreal, Cincinnati, and Boston. Sharperson was also drafted in the first round of the 1981 draft, by the Toronto Blue Jays.

"When we first got started, we'd play against each other in spring training for Orangeburg bragging rights," Winningham said. "If I made a play to get him out, I had bragging rights. If he got me out, he had bragging rights. After we both made it to the majors, we'd always get together for dinner and talk about how we got where we wanted to go and that you couldn't go any further than this."

Sharperson wasn't a star, but in 1992 he represented the Los Angeles Dodgers in the All-Star Game. A solid, dependable utility infielder, he enjoyed his lone .300 season in L.A., earning a spot in Baseball's Summer Classic. He and Lenny Harris became a strong combo at third base for the Dodgers that year, each bringing talent and enthusiasm to the Los Angeles infield.

"Sharpie was a wonderful role player who was always working hard, trying to become a regular, everyday player," said his former teammate, relief pitcher Jim Gott. "While he might not have had Alex Rodriguez talent, he always had an Alex Rodriguez heart. He was a great guy. He was the judge in our Kangaroo Court. He would wear an old wig and use a baseball bat as a gavel."

After signing with Toronto, Sharperson played his first two seasons with Florence and Kingston of the Carolina Leagues, where he hit in the mid-200s. But after being promoted to Knoxville of the

Southern League in 1984, the 22-year-old became a top prospect with a .304 average. During each of the next two seasons, he hit .289 for Syracuse of the International League and was hitting the ball at a .299 clip in 1987 when he was recalled by Toronto. Hitting just .208 in 32 games for the Blue Jays, he was traded to the Dodgers on September 22 in exchange for pitcher Juan Guzman. Finishing out the season with the Dodgers, he hit .273 in 10 games.

He split the 1988 season with Triple A Albuquerque of the Pacific Coast League hitting .319 and the Dodgers, where he hit .271 in 46 games.

The following season saw him up and down with Los Angeles until he made it to stay in 1990, hitting a solid .297 in 129 games. During the next two seasons, he hit .278 and .300 respectively. It appeared that the 1992 All-Star had finally arrived in the major leagues as a steady, if not spectacular, player.

"He was a gutsy guy who would get in front of the balls hit to him at third base," said Jim Gott. "He would never ole' the ball. Sharpie had an incredible work ethic. He made the most of his talent. As hard as he worked, he always smiled because he really appreciated what he had. He was so much fun. He'd always make you laugh as he threw the ball back to you on the mound from third base."

Two years after his All Star season, Mike Sharperson once again found himself toiling and riding buses in the minor leagues, playing in places such as Pawtucket, Rhode Island, Iowa, and Richmond, Virginia.

"I always pulled for Mike and he always pulled for me," said Herm Winningham. "He was a very versatile player who could play a lot of positions. He was a better ballplayer than I was.

"He was a very caring person who didn't pull any punches. He was wild, but in a very good sense. We always got together and our moms always spoke quite often back home."

At the age of 34 Sharperson was hitting .304 for Las Vegas in the Pacific Coast League, hoping for one more shot at the major leagues. The call came and he was just hours away from joining the San Diego

Padres as an early-season call-up. But as he drove home early in the morning of May 26, 1996, Mike Sharperson was killed in a one-car crash. Alcohol was not a factor in the accident. Following a get-together with his Las Vegas teammates, he was traveling southbound on I-15 and reacted too slowly in his attempt to turn onto I-215 to go home, probably to pack for his return to the major leagues. He lost control of his car on the rain-slicked highway and hit a dirt median.

Taken to the University Medical Center, he died on the operating table at 5:15 A.M., ending his dream of once again returning to the major leagues just hours before it would have been realized.

"They just told him that he was being recalled to the Padres," said Winningham. "He was going back to pack to join the team in Montreal, where they were playing when it happened. It's just tragic. I was always proud of him and I still am. We miss him. I see his brother and his mother all the time. His work on Earth was done and the Lord took him. At least that's how I look at it.

"When I think about Mike, I think mostly about our childhood and when we played on the same teams in high school and college. I'm just glad that I got to know him."

CHICO RUIZ

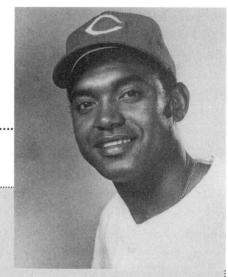

Courtesy of the Cincinnati Reds.

California Angels
Infielder

Bats: Both; Throws: Right
Height: 6 ft.;
   Weight: 173 lbs.

Born: December 5, 1938, in Santo Domingo, Cuba
Died: February 9, 1972, in San Diego, Calif.

Acquired by the California Angels from the Cincinnati Reds
   with Alex Johnson for Jim McGlothlin, Vern Geisher, and
   Pedro Borbon.
8 Seasons   .240 BA   2 HR   69 RBIs

HIS STEAL OF HOME PLATE
ALTERED A PENNANT RACE

Hiraldo Ruiz Sablon, better known as Chico Ruiz, was a serviceable
major league utility infielder for eight seasons in the 1960s and early
1970s, primarily with the Cincinnati Reds. Toward the end of his
career he also played for the California Angels.

   Although he never played in more than 105 games, he was a
valuable bench player who could come in on a moment's notice to

pinch hit, or play on the field. In his final season of 1971, Chico Ruiz had his highest career batting average when he hit .263 for the Angels. While in his major league career, Chico Ruiz amassed just 34 stolen bases; he was known as a prolific base stealer in the minors. While he swiped but 34 bases in his big league career, one particular steal made him the stuff of legend in a town where he was only a visiting player.

The year was 1964 and it was called, "The Year of the Blue Snow," by Philadelphia Phillies veteran catcher Gus Triandos. That was the season in which the Phillies mounted an improbable run for the National League pennant. With a seemingly insurmountable six-and-one-half game lead with just 10 games left to play, the 14-year drought since the 1950 Whiz Kids appeared in the World Series appeared to be over. In the City of Brotherly Love, World Series tickets were already being printed. But a funny thing happened on the way to the Fall Classic—Chico Ruiz.

On September 21, the first-place Phillies hosted the second-place Reds. A pair of right-handers, Art Mahaffey of the Phillies and John Tsitouris of Cincinnati, hooked up in a scoreless pitcher's duel. In the sixth inning of the contest, Ruiz hit a single to right field. Vada Pinson then hit a line drive to right field for a hit, but was thrown out by Phillies strong-armed right fielder Johnny Callison as Pinson tried to stretch a single into a double.

With two outs and Ruiz at third base, the hitter was future Hall of Famer Frank Robinson. Mahaffey had a one strike count and went into his windup as Chico Ruiz broke for home. Mahaffey uncorked a wild pitch past catcher Clay Dalrymple, allowing Ruiz to score what turned out to be the only run of the contest.

"With Frank Robinson at the plate, no one in the world would have expected him [Ruiz] to steal home," said Jack Baldschun, the closer on the '64 Phillies team who later pitched for Cincinnati. "Art Mahaffey was into his windup when everybody started yelling, 'There he goes.'

"But instead of brushing Robinson back or throwing the pitch inside, Mahaffey threw it low and away and Ruiz scored."

The Phillies went on to blow the pennant, losing nine of their last 11 games, and finishing in third place. To this day, the name "Ruiz" is truly a four-letter word in Philadelphia.

The 25-year-old rookie hit .244 for the Reds that season, stealing a total of 11 bases in 77 games. Signed as an amateur free agent, Ruiz began his professional career with Geneva of the NY-PA league hitting .251 in 126 games.

He showed steady improvement as he advanced through the Reds farm system hitting .283, .298, and .314 in successive years playing for San Diego of the Pacific Coast League. But a solid lineup in Cincinnati and major league pitching relegated him to duty as a utility player.

"Chico was a helluva nice guy," said Jack Baldschun. "He was a good teammate and was always rooting for the team. Like the rest of us, he was just happy to be there. Chico used to have a little cushion that he'd bring out and put on the bench to sit on. He knew that he wasn't going to get in the game unless he replaced somebody or pinch hit, so he always would sit on his little cushion."

After six years with the Reds, prior to the 1970 season, he was dealt to the California Angels along with Alex Johnson in exchange for pitchers Jim McGlothlin, Vern Geishert, and Pedro Borbon. Ruiz hit .243 for the Angels, appearing in 68 games.

On June 17 of the following season, he was involved in an incident with teammate Johnson, allegedly pulling a gun on the burly outfielder. There were no witnesses to the incident, which Ruiz denied. General Manager Dick Walsh first denied the incident ever occurred, but then changed his story when he appeared in front of an arbitration panel that had been called to discuss a possible suspension of Johnson.

Ruiz went on to hit .263 that season in just 31 games. The incident in question seemed to be a departure from the happy, friendly player that was known throughout baseball.

"He was an excellent ballplayer," said former Pirates catcher Jim Pagliaroni. "A great hustler who was a 110 percent type of guy. That comes from an attitude of being grateful for what you have. That attitude stands out. You don't look at yourself as something special. That's what he was like. If you have a joyful heart, you know you've been blessed with what you have."

The professional career of Chico Ruiz had hit a rut. Let go by the Angels, he was assigned to their farm club in Salt Lake City. Following the 1971 season, he was placed on the Class A Davenport, Iowa, roster.

But all was not lost as he was scheduled to report to the Kansas City Royals training camp, under contract to their Triple A farm club in Omaha. Team officials felt certain that the veteran infielder would earn a spot on the major league roster.

But prior to spring training, on February 9, 1972, Chico Ruiz was killed when the car he was driving on Interstate 5 in San Diego hit a sign pole. He was driving at a high rate of speed when the accident occurred and was pronounced dead on arrival at Palomar Hospital, near San Diego.

Chico Ruiz played eight seasons in the major leagues, but will forever be best remembered for his inexplicable steal of home plate in a game that began the slide of the 1964 Philadelphia Phillies.

Just one month prior to his death, Ruiz had become a naturalized U.S. citizen.

PLAYERS WHO DIED
OF NATURAL CAUSES

any of us spend the first part of our lives trying to get the things we want. Then, we spend the rest of our lives trying to keep what we have. But the truth of the matter is that if we don't have our health, we don't have anything.

We've all had loved ones, friends, or coworkers who have had a fatal heart attack, or who have contracted a fatal disease. Telethons and statistics can be very comfortable until our family or circle of friends have become part of a national head count. Most of us live quiet lives out of the limelight, and when we pass away, the occasion is rarely marked with huge fanfare.

But when a celebrity dies, or confides that he or she is battling a fatal disease, the public attention on the unfortunate person's problems can often be blown way out of proportion.

Of course, the typical sports fan realizes that the baseball players whose careers we follow summer after summer are just mere mortals. But if only they would swing and miss just a little more often, it would be easier to believe that they really are just like the rest of us.

And then, one of them dies.

Most recently, the untimely death of St. Louis Cardinals pitcher Darryl Kile knocked baseball, and the entire sports world, on its ear.

He was young, strong, vibrant, talented, and popular. With the suddenness of a bolt of lightening, he was gone.

Any Bostonian who was of the age of reason in the 1950s can surely recount the sad story of the Golden Greek, Harry Agganis. He was an outstanding baseball player and a superlative football player who was sought after by colleges all over the country. But the home boy picked Boston University to a large degree so that his widowed mother could see his games in person. Just two years after his pro baseball career began, he was dead. And the children of the aforementioned generation of Boston natives and fans have heard the story of Harry Agganis almost since birth.

Walt Bond, a monstrously powerful giant of a man who starred with the Houston Astros and a gifted former All-American shortstop named Danny Thompson were both taken at the age of 29 from leukemia. Both continued to play major league baseball to a high level after being diagnosed with the killer disease, only to fade quickly when the leukemia reached its deadly stage.

Bond's teammate with the Astros, pitcher Jim Umbricht fought a courageous battle against cancer, and after undergoing surgery, he often was in pain and bleeding when he pitched. His story took a heartbreaking turn during the season when he learned that his cancer was going to kill him. He died the next winter, but Big Jim, as he was known, may have one of the biggest headstones in the country.

Young Dick Wantz suffered from severe headaches for years. But after he cracked the California Angels pitching staff, the headaches grew progressively worse. After a short stay in a Detroit hospital and an initial misdiagnosis, brain cancer was discovered and surgery proved unsuccessful. Dick Wantz died one month to the day he made his major league debut . . . and his only big league appearance.

HARRY AGGANIS

Harry Agganis, left, with Boston University coach "Buff" Donelli.
Courtesy of Boston University.

Boston Red Sox
First Base

Bats: Left; Throws: Left
Height: 6 ft. 2 in.; Weight: 200 lbs.

Born: April 20, 1929, in Lynn, Mass.
Died: June 27, 1955, in Cambridge, Mass.

Signed as an amateur free agent by the Boston Red Sox
  in 1953.
2 Seasons   .261 BA   11 HR   67 RBIs   8 SB

THE GREATEST BOSTON
ATHLETE NEVER TO BE

All sports franchises will sooner or later have to endure the tragic loss
of a player to an accident, illness, or some other unfortunate end. But
love them or hate them, no one can deny that the Boston Red Sox
have had more than their share of sad stories involving some of their
Bosox players over the years.

Tragic happenings involving Beantown athletes include Big Ed
Morris, who had the misfortune of being stabbed to death at a party
held in his honor. The Bay State's favorite son, Tony Conigliaro, a
young, budding superstar had his career cut short after being beaned
by Angels pitcher Jack Hamilton. Then, after struggling to find himself following the premature end to his career, Conigliaro suffered a
debilitating heart attack following an interview to become a Red Sox
announcer. He died years later.

Young basketball star Len Bias died of a drug overdose shortly
after becoming the first-round draft pick of the Boston Celtics. But
few stories rocked the Bay State more than the passing of Red Sox
first baseman Harry Agganis in 1955 at the age of 25. He is sometimes referred to as the greatest Boston athlete never to be.

Nicknamed "The Golden Greek," Aristotle George Agganis was
born in Lynn, Mass., and became a two-sport star at Boston
University, playing both football and baseball. Ironically, his accomplishments on the gridiron fields gained Harry Agganis most of his
notoriety.

His football exploits at Classical High School in Lynn had college scouts from across the country drooling with eager anticipation. During his three-year hitch in high school, Agganis led Classical to a 30-4-1 record. His individual statistics were even more impressive, as he threw for 48 touchdowns, ran for 24 more, and threw for a total of 4,149 yards. Not bad for a high school kid.

As a sophomore quarterback at Boston University, in 1949, he set a school record by throwing 15 touchdown passes. Following a brief stint in the Marine Corps, he returned to school and became Boston University's first All-American in football. He threw for a total of 34 touchdowns in his college career, good enough for third place on the BU QB list.

But this was no typical high school or college performer, Harry Agganis was the Golden Greek.

After setting what was at the time a college passing record with 1,402 yards in his senior year, Agganis was drafted in the first round of the NFL draft by the Cleveland Browns. Coach Paul Brown envisioned the lefty QB as his future signal caller. But baseball was the true love of Harry Agganis and he spurned the Browns offer and signed with the Red Sox following his college graduation in 1953.

Assigned to the Sox Triple A farm club in Louisville, the slugging first baseman didn't miss a beat hitting at a .281 clip with 23 home runs and 108 RBIs.

The following season, in 1954, he would get his shot at The Show. In spring training of that year, Harry Agganis and Billy Consolo met for the first time when the club assigned them as roommates while in the Grapefruit League.

"Harry had signed before I did," said Consolo, who played 10 major league seasons. "He was my first roommate in baseball. They told me that he was a quarterback for BU. I was just a kid out of high school and I expected to see a guy who was maybe 5-foot-10 and 180 pounds. We stayed at the John Ringling Hotel and when I walked into the hotel room, Harry was in the bathroom shaving. He walked out and he was, The Golden Greek, an incredible hunk of a man. I had no idea that he was an All-American football player. He had so many different clothes and shoes that I didn't have any room for my stuff in the closet.

"He was the best competitor I ever saw. He had been a football player first. We were together every night for 35 days until he went to Louisville. I think Paul Brown of the Cleveland Browns must have called him about 15 times trying to get him to play for his team. Otto Graham was going to retire and he wanted Harry to replace him."

Following his outstanding season at Louisville, Agganis became a regular with the Red Sox and had what was considered a disappointing rookie campaign. He hit .251 with 11 homers and 57 RBIs, all figures that were considered below his ability and potential, but more than respectable for a rookie in the major leagues. While his rookie season was certainly not a bad one, expectations for The Golden Greek were quite high. But the experience of that first season helped prepare Harry Agganis for the 1955 season, and he was determined to make it a better one, where he would make his mark at Fenway Park for his baseball exploits. It was the same stadium where he had played so many football games for BU.

Rookie Norm Zauchin was the starting first sacker as the season began for Boston, but Agganis quickly took the position back. Through 25 games, he was hitting .313 and appeared to be rebounding from his frustrating freshman year and on his way to a long, successful big league career. But sadly, that was not to be the case.

Agganis was hospitalized for more than a week beginning May 16 with a chest ailment. He had complained of chest pains and had a high fever. After treatment, he was well enough to return to the lineup. He played on June 1 and 2, but was stricken again with the same chest ailment in Kansas City and reentered the hospital on June 5.

Just three weeks later, he was dead. Agganis had been making a slow, but satisfying recovery from the severe pulmonary infection, which was complicated by phlebitis. But he died of a massive pulmonary embolism, caused by a clot or obstruction in the flow of blood to the lung.

"My mother called me and told me that she had heard about Harry's death," Billy Consolo said. "I was shocked and I didn't know what happened. After he died I wanted to go to his funeral, but it was during the season and I wasn't able to go. I still get choked up just thinking about it.

"As a player he was a comer who was getting better all the time. He played first base in '54. He was a big, strong guy who hit line drives. He was ready to do something in the big leagues and everybody liked him."

Former Red Sox catcher Jim Pagliaroni, an 11-year major league veteran, commented, "He was just a wonderful human being. From everyone who has ever met him, you hear about how much he was loved by his community. He was great with people and great with kids. You can't imagine how upset people were when they heard that he had died."

What he would have accomplished had he lived will forever remain a mystery. But aside from the human tragedy, his death also represents a glowing example of lost potential.

"The way he hit line drives, the power would have come later," said Bill Consolo. "He was just a marvelous man. He would have been a helluva player for the Red Sox for a lot of years. He had it all. I think he would have had a career much like Carl Yastrzemski, who also had a little bit of a tough time when he first played in Boston."

When Harry Agganis died, the city of Boston mourned en masse. More than 10,000 people attended his funeral at St. George's Greek Orthodox Church in Lynn. It was also estimated that another 20,000 lined the route from the church to his final resting place in Pine Grove Cemetery.

He is now a member of the College Football Hall of Fame, and the Red Sox honored him in 1995 by renaming Gaffney Street in Boston Harry Agganis Way.

FRANCISCO BARRIOS

Chicago White Sox
Pitcher

Bats: Right; Throws: Right
Height: 6 ft. 3 in.; Weight: 195 lbs.

Born: June 10, 1953, in Hermosillo, Sonora, Mexico
Died: April 9, 1982, in Hermosillo, Senora, Mexico

Traded by Jalisco of the Mexican League with Manuel Lugo
to the Chicago White Sox for Rudy Hernandez on
December 4, 1973.

7 Seasons   38 Wins   38 Losses   4.15 ERA

A CAREER DERAILED BY A
SORE ARM AND A WEAK HEART

During his seven-year major league career, Francisco Barrios was
known as a great competitor on the playing field and a fun teammate
off the field. Making a name for himself as a young, fire-balling right-
hander in the Mexican League in the early 1970s, he had a 10-12
season with Jalisco in 1973, which saw the 20-year-old get a brief
look-see with Phoenix, the Pacific Coast League AAA team of the
San Francisco Giants, and was then released.

That winter the young pitcher was acquired by the Chicago White
Sox where it was felt he would have a chance to show his stuff. He put

together a strong 9-5 campaign for Knoxville of the Southern League with a 3.92 ERA which earned him a two-game stint in Chicago.

It was back to Jalisco in 1975 where he once again had a 10-12 record with an impressive 2.70 ERA, allowing just 169 hits in 183 innings. He finished the year 2-0 with Denver of the American Association. It was obvious that the young hurler would be a prominent member of the ChiSox staff the following season.

Barrios went 5-9 for the White Sox in 1976 with a 4.31 ERA. But that full season of big league experience enabled Barrios to prepare himself for his best pro season in 1977 in which he boasted a 14-7 record with a 4.13 ERA in 231 innings. In 1978 he went 9-15 for Chicago, but pitched better than his record indicated. He was earning the reputation of a dependable starter who gave his club a chance to win most any game he pitched.

He spent six weeks on the disabled list the following season with arm problems, but still managed to have an 8-3 record with a 3.60 ERA in 15 games.

Rotator cuff surgery limited his availability to just three games with a 1-1 record in 1980. But in addition to the hard work he put in to rehabilitating his arm, Barrios began to play hard off the field as well. In 1981, he had a fistfight with good friend, pitcher Steve Trout and was arrested in a drug bust. The talented righty enrolled in a drug abuse rehabilitation program in an effort to get his life straightened out.

But the injury history and the other blemishes on his behavioral record combined to cause his release by the White Sox in September of that year. Rather than mope about the situation, Barrios returned to Mexico and pitched for his hometown team, the Hermosillo Orange-Pickers. He had five shutouts in six games and had agreed to sign a contract with the Milwaukee Brewers.

But then his arm began bothering him again, and Francisco Barrios died of a heart attack at the home of his parents on April 8, 1982. His former teammates were shocked and saddened by his death because Frankie, as he was known, was such a popular player.

He left behind a wife and five-year-old daughter.

STEVE BECHLER

Baltimore Orioles
Pitcher

Bats: Right; Throws: Right
Height: 6 ft. 4 in.; Weight: 225 lbs.

Born: November 18, 1979, in Medford, Ore.
Died: February 17, 2003, in Ft. Lauderdale, Fla.

Drafted in the third round of the 1998 amateur draft by the
    Baltimore Orioles.
1 Season   0 Wins   0 Losses   13.50 ERA

A PREVENTABLE DEATH

In 2003 Steve Bechler seemed to have many of the health concerns
many other men shared. He was overweight, out of shape, on a diet,
and not eating properly in an attempt to lose some pounds. He also
had high blood pressure. But where he differed from many with similar conditions, Bechler was just 23 years old and trying to make the
Baltimore Orioles pitching staff.

Coming off his first taste of big league action at the end of the
2002 season in which he had three appearances with the Orioles,
Bechler was in an uphill fight to make the big league roster the following spring. While not used to the hot and humid weather in
Florida, he continued to work hard in an attempt to get himself into

shape. But it appears that the final ingredient in this tragic puzzle was the pitcher's decision to take an over-the-counter supplement containing ephedrine, a stimulant that aids in weight loss and boosts performance.

It is believed that Steve Bechler took three of these pills on an empty stomach. On February 17, following a workout, his temperature soared to 108 degrees. He died at the North Ridge Medical Center in Fort Lauderdale from heat stroke. The official autopsy spoke of the young prospect's assortment of potentially dangerous medical problems, along with his desperate attempts to lose weight. It is believed that the heat stroke was brought on by a number of factors, including an enlarged heart, abnormal liver function, borderline hypertension, being overweight, and using a diet supplement that played a "significant role in his death."

The medical examiner of Broward County reported that "the ephedra raised his body temperature, leading to heat stroke. And it was not a particular strenuous exercise carried out and not on a particularly hot day." He further said that Bechler died of multiple organ failure and with a temperature of 108 degrees. A toxicology examination showed a significant amount of ephedra was discovered in Bechler's system.

While not banned by Major League Baseball, the diet supplement in question was banned by the National Football League, the NCAA, and the Olympic Committee.

The untimely death of Steve Bechler brought to an end the career of a young pitcher who had risen steadily through the Baltimore minor league system. Sporting a fastball in the low-90s and a good knuckle curveball, he saw his first professional action in 1998 when he was the third-round pick of the Orioles in the amateur draft. Bechler pitched in nine games for Gulf Coast, with a 2-4 record and a fine ERA of 2.72. Exhibiting good command of his pitches, he struck out 39 batters while walking just eight.

In 1999, his first full season as a pro, Steve Bechler pitched in 26 games for Delmarva, with an 8-12 record and a 3.54 ERA. He again showed good control by walking only 58 while striking out 139 batters in 152 innings.

Bechler was promoted to the Frederick Keys for the 2000 campaign and he continued to impress with an 8-12 mark and a 4.83 ERA in 162 innings. Even though he endured losing seasons, he continued to impress with his mound presence. In 2001, he got off to an excellent start at Frederick with a 5-2 record. He was 3-5 at Bowie and 1-1 with Triple A Rochester.

The following season saw Bechler get off to a horrible start with the Red Wings before pitching well en route to a 6-11 record. His strong latter half of the season earned him a promotion to the Orioles, where he pitched in three games out of the Baltimore bullpen. But after working his way through the organization and getting a taste of the big leagues, spring training 2003 was an important time in Steve Bechler's career.

Unfortunately, it was also the time of his tragic death.

Following the incident, Kiley Bechler, Steve's widow, filed a $600 million lawsuit against the manufacturers of the product, Nutraquest Inc. There was a settlement of nearly one million dollars.

WALT BOND

Walt Bond, left, with Joe Gaines.

Courtesy of Donald Bond.

Minnesota Twins
Outfield/First Base

Bats: Left; Throws: Right
Height: 6 ft. 7 in.; Weight: 228 lbs.

Born: October 19, 1937, in Denmark, Tenn.
Died: September 14, 1967, in Houston, Tex.

Sent from the Houston Astros to the Minnesota Twins prior to the 1966 season.

6 Seasons   .256 BA   41 HR   179 RBIs

A PLAYER WHO WAGED
A BRAVE BATTLE AGAINST
A RELENTLESS ILLNESS

Walt Bond was a giant of a man. His 6 feet 7 inch frame coupled with a muscular 228 pounds made him an imposing figure in the batter's box. As one might expect, he possessed plenty of power when he stepped up to the left-hand side of the plate.

"He was a big, strong silent type of guy," said Tal Smith, Houston Astros president of baseball operations. "He played first base and outfield. He was your typical first baseman who was big, tall, and strong. Power was his primary tool. He hit with a lot of power before he got ill."

Astro's outfielder Jimmy Wynn was a close friend. "Walt was a very good ballplayer," he said. "He handled himself very well. He wasn't what you'd expect. He was very laid back for a big man. But his career and life were cut short by leukemia."

For those who remember Walt Bond, there always seemed to be two continuing story lines during his career: The strong, almost Herculean build, which helped produce mammoth home runs, and then there were the whispers. Rumors circulated around baseball that he was suffering from leukemia. It was a rumor Bond flatly denied as he wanted to concentrate on being the best baseball player he could be.

"In the 1960s, cancer was the 'Big C' word, much like you have the 'Big A' word in today's world," said Bond's son Donald, who is a CPA in Houston. "There was a stigma about it. If someone had cancer, could you catch it from them? In those days, the clubs didn't want a player on the team who had such a disease. They didn't want the responsibility. Then in the 1970s, people got very open about the disease.

"He was not a complainer. He felt that he could beat it. He probably found out about it in 1958 when he was in the service and lived until 1967 and that was without all of the wonder drugs you have today. His athleticism and the shape he kept himself in probably prolonged his life.

"He didn't dwell on it."

While Walt Bond didn't want to dwell on leukemia, there were times in his career when he was traded or let go by a team for no apparent reason. All he wanted was the chance to play baseball, something he no doubt earned with his minor league credentials. And whenever that opportunity presented itself, he responded quite impressively.

"He was a little upset with the game," Donald Bond commented. "There were some issues with racism, what black ballplayers went through as opposed to the white players. He actually had a greater love of basketball. But some of the baseball teams were after his brother, Willie Bond, who got my dad to go to a tryout with him.

"I can remember when he taught me how to throw a baseball. He was gripping it across the seams. He would tell me that the seams were the steering wheel of the ball."

A native of Denmark, Tenn., Bond signed his first professional contract with the St. Louis Cardinals in 1955 and then became property of the Kansas City Monarchs, who sold him to the Cleveland Indians. He had three good seasons in the Tribe system, hitting .328 with Cocoa of the Florida State League in 1957 with 11 home runs and 80 RBIs. He followed up that year with a solid season playing for Burlington in the Carolina League, hitting .296, smacking 13 home runs while driving in 70. Playing with Reading of the Eastern League in 1959, the young slugger continued to put up impressive numbers. That season he hit .277 with 16 home runs, knocking in 82.

But it was in 1960 that Bond's solid minor league seasons began to pay dividends for him. Hitting .318 with Vancouver of the Pacific Coast League with 12 home runs and 45 RBIs in 74 games, Bond earned a much deserved call-up to the Cleveland Indians. In his first

40 big league games, he hit just .221 with five homers and 18 RBIs. But he was clearly a top-notch prospect who gained vitally useful experience with the Tribe, learning the differences between major and minor league pitching.

He split the 1961 season going between Triple A Salt Lake City and Cleveland. With Salt Lake, he hit for a solid .283 average with 8 homers and 37 RBIs in 70 games. Seeing limited action following his recall to Cleveland, he hit just .173 in 38 games.

The same scenario played out in 1962 as Bond played a full minor league season in Salt Lake City, hitting .320 with 11 home runs and 76 RBIs. He may have been disappointed with the lack of playing time with the Indians, but rather than mope in Triple A, Bond continued to put up impressive numbers. In a late-season call-up by Cleveland, he was limited to 12 games, hitting .380.

Although he always denied that he had leukemia, during a military stint, Bond had a hernia corrected in 1962. He was suffering from Myelogeous leukemia. It was treated for nearly three months and went into a state of remission. The Cleveland organization sent him to the Western Reserve school of medicine. There he received the same sad news, although at least the disease was in a state of arrest with no detectable progression. It is thought that since he felt well and was able to play baseball at a high level that Bond did not really accept the fact that he had the disease. He felt fine and was still a very productive player who felt he had a long career and life in front of him. It retrospect, it was probably natural to doubt the diagnosis, particularly since when in remission those with leukemia quite often feel normal and healthy.

He spent the entire 1963 season with Jacksonville of the International League, hitting .276 with 25 home runs and 82 RBIs. Whispers of a serious illness or not, Bond was purchased by the Houston Colt .45s in December of that year. Apparently the Cleveland organization was uncomfortable with Bond's situation; plus, he needed a chance to play regularly. Houston would provide him that opportunity.

His breakout season came in 1964 when he played in 148 games for the Astros, hitting for a .254 average, smacking 20 homers and driving in a then Houston record 85 runs. Walt Bond had arrived and the sky appeared the limit. All the years of frustration of playing in the minor leagues had paid off and the big slugger had made quite a splash in the National League.

The following season his production slipped. Was it the typical sophomore jinx, or was it something more serious? He still played in 117 games with 407 at bats and his batting average improved to .263. But he hit only seven home runs and drove in 47. There were times he appeared sluggish and was having problems misplaying batted balls in the outfield.

Prior to the start of the 1966 season, and with details unknown, Bond was shipped to the Minnesota Twins. With Chuck Harrison and Jim Gentile available, Houston brass decided they had enough left-handed bats. The Twins sent him to the Triple A Denver Bears, where he had another solid season as a pinch hitter and part-time outfielder/first baseman.

Bond was back in the bigs in 1967 as a utility player and pinch hitter with Minnesota. In 10 games, he hit .312 with one homer and five RBIs. But then, for no apparent reason, he was released on May 15. The Mets seemingly dangled one last chance in front of Bond, but the opportunity disappeared.

His health was deteriorating fairly rapidly and he spent most of the summer of 1967 in the Houston Medical Center. On September 14, just more than four months after his final major league game, Walt Bond died.

"I don't know if he knew he was dying," said Donald Bond. "I never heard him dwell on it. He knew he was sick. If he knew he was dying, I think he refused to believe it. I was 12 when he passed. He told me to be a man. Had he lived, he would not have pushed me toward athletics. Like other players of his era, during the off-season, he had a regular job. I still remember him tying his tie. But he said to be a man, to be honest and be true to yourself.

"To this day, I come across people who met my dad and tell me what a nice man he was. I go through life trying to fill those shoes."

Bond was known for his charitable work in the Houston area and always seemed to make an impression on others because of the type of person he was. Bond not only knew how to live, but he also knew how to die with dignity.

One of his doctors, Hatch W. Cummings Jr., the chief of internal medicine services at the Texas Medical Center, wrote the following letter to a Houston newspaper and sent a copy to the Bond family. It is this communication that finally answered the questions of Walt Bond's health and gives great insight into his mental strength, denying the disease and attempting to defeat it with sheer will power.

"During the several years that I have known Walter, I have liked him as a person and respected him as a man," wrote Dr. Cummings. "It has been my sad duty to stand by and help when I could, while a strong, proud man succumbed to a relentless disease.

"He was of an age when he should have been at the peak of his physical power and when the combativeness and aggressiveness of baseball should have been its natural expression, yet he had been found to have a disease that would relentlessly destroy him. One that would smolder along, in such an occult and subtle way, that even the experienced observer would doubt its presence, and then it would strike him down with a rapidity that would remind one of the rapier blade.

"Although I feel certain that Walter was aware of this relentless nature of his disease, he appeared unwilling to consider the situation so hopeless, but that by some great effort of the will, it could be changed. I had felt it my duty to inform him of its seriousness. The medical examination left no doubt of the grave prognosis. To the surprise of myself and the other physicians involved, there was no need for active treatment during the two years that Walter was with the Houston baseball club. There were moments when I might have doubted the diagnosis myself, had we not taken great pains to make certain of it in the beginning, so that it was not difficult to understand Walter's apparent reluctance, at times, to accept the validity of the diagnosis.

"In the early part of this summer (1967), it was apparent that the dreaded conversion to an acute terminal phase had occurred. From that time until his death, his illness was progressive and unyielding. It was obvious that we were waging a losing battle to control it, but Walter never ceased to fight. He never gave up. He showed the strength of character and will that only champions possess. It was an exhibition of courage, and in the best tradition of baseball."

Walt Bond defied death to the very end. That the disease that killed him allowed him to live a normal life as a professional baseball player was in some ways a cruel diversion from the ultimate end that he could not change, even with his incredible will power.

Donald Bond has had some big shoes to fill in his lifetime. But you get the impression that his father would be as proud of him as Donald is of his father.

ERNIE "TINY" BONHAM

Courtesy of the Pittsburgh Pirates.

Pittsburgh Pirates
Pitcher

Bats: Right; Throws: Right
Height: 6 ft. 2 in.; Weight: 215 lbs.

Born: August 13, 1913, in Ione, Calif.
Died: September 15, 1949, in Pittsburgh, Pa.

Traded by the New York Yankees to the Pittsburgh Pirates for
Cookie Cuccurollo on October 24, 1946.
10 Seasons   103 Wins   72 Losses   4.01 ERA

HIS RETIREMENT DREAMS
WERE NEVER MEANT TO BE

Veteran Pittsburgh Pirates right-hander Ernie "Tiny" Bonham was
pretty much ready to call it a career following the 1949 season. In his
10 big league seasons, Bonham had been to three consecutive World
Series with the New York Yankees, capturing the championship
twice. But worn down by years of arm and back miseries, followed by
losing seasons with the Pirates, had him ready to hang up the spikes
after the season and enjoy his retirement.

On August 28, 1949, Bonham pitched the Pirates past the
Philadelphia Phillies, earning his sixth straight decision and improving his record to 7-4. On September 8, after complaining of abdom-
inal pain, he was admitted to Pittsburgh Presbyterian Hospital. An
appendectomy was performed and surgeons were also said to have
learned he was suffering from intestinal cancer. He died a week later
of what doctors described as irreversible shock and cardiovascular
failure.

His wife, Ruth, and a Catholic priest were at his bedside at the
time of his passing. Mrs. Bonham was the first baseball widow to

receive a death benefit under the baseball pension plan, receiving $90 a month for 10 years.

Bonham's death marked the end of a life filled with accomplishment that few might have expected. He was the 13th of 14 children born in his family. Bonham was born in the farming community of Ione, Calif., in 1913 and earned the nickname "Tiny" because of his hefty size. He was certainly not fat; rather, he was large and muscular. This was in no small part due to the fact that, as a young man, he did a great deal of hard, physical labor. In addition to working on the family farm, he also worked on the Oakland docks and in a lumber yard.

Signed by the New York Yankees organization in 1935, "Tiny" Bonham rose quickly through the farm system, playing for teams in Modesto, Akron, Binghamton, and Oakland, where he hurled a no-hitter against Seattle in 1937.

With the parent New York Yankees club struggling through most of the 1940 season, in August Manager Joe "Skipper" McCarthy summoned the stocky 26-year-old pitcher to bolster his sagging pitching staff. Bonham responded with a 9-3 record in 12 games with a glittering 1.90 ERA. The highlight of the season for the rookie hurler had to be on September 19 when he out-dueled Bobby Feller, pitching the Yankees into a short-lived visit to first place. Following the season, "Skipper" McCarthy told reporters that his team would have captured the pennant had Bonham been with the team all season.

Sporting a better than average fastball, Bonham's out pitch was the forkball. In fact, he is believed to be the first pitcher to regularly use the pitch. But throughout his career, he suffered with chronic back pain that, at times, limited his effectiveness, particularly near the end of his career.

His first year in the major leagues was quite a season as the Yankees captured the World Series, with Bonham pitching the decisive game in the Fall Classic, a 3-1 decision over the Brooklyn Dodgers and their ace hurler, Whitlow Wyatt. During the regular season, he had a 9-6 record with a fine 2.98 ERA.

Bonham became a big-time pitcher in 1942, sporting a 21-5 record with a league-leading winning percentage of .808. He also was a league leader in complete games with 22, and shutouts with 6, throwing a career high 226 innings with an ERA of 2.27. Selected to the American League All-Star team, Bonham did not pitch.

The Bronx Bombers returned to the World Series that fall, but were defeated by the St. Louis Cardinals, four games to one. Bonham pitched in two games with a 0-1 record.

But the 1943 season ended with a third consecutive trip to the Series for the Yankees, who beat St. Louis by a 4-1 margin. Although Bonham was 0-1 in that Series, he put together another outstanding season in New York, going 15-8, with a 2.27 ERA in 225 innings. Once again, he was selected to the All-Star Game.

With the country at war, Bonham went to the draft board only to be designated 4-F because of his back problems. So, while he was unable to join the service like so many other players of the era, "Tiny" Bonham continued to toil for the Yankees. But his sore back began to play a more dominant role in his career. The 1944 season saw the 30-year-old slip to a 12-9 record, albeit with a respectable 2.99 ERA. But for the first time in his major league career, he allowed more hits than innings pitched.

The trend continued during the 1945 season as his record slipped to 8-11 and his ERA rose to 3.19. After going just 5-8 with the '46 Yanks, "Tiny" Bonham was traded following the season to Pittsburgh in exchange for pitcher Cookie Cuccurollo.

The veteran forkball specialist had an encouraging year for the Bucs in 1947, winning 11, while losing eight as a spot starter and reliever, with a 3.85 ERA in 149 innings pitched. The 1948 season saw him pitch to a 6-10 record with a 4.31 ERA.

Bonham pitched well for Pittsburgh in the months before his death. Pirates Manager Billy Meyer was particularly upset over the pitcher's death as he had been Bonham's manager going back as far back as 1936 with Binghamton of the New York-Pennsylvania League.

HAL
CARLSON

Courtesy of the Baseball Hall of Fame.

Chicago Cubs
Pitcher

Bats: Right; Throws: Right
Height: 6 ft.;
    Weight: 180 lbs.

Born: May 17, 1892,
    in Rockford, Ill.
Died: May 28, 1930,
    in Chicago, Ill.

Traded by the Philadelphia Phillies to the Chicago Cubs
    in exchange for Tony Kaufmann and Jimmy Cooney on
    June 27, 1927.
14 Seasons   114 Wins   120 Losses   3.97 ERA

DIED SUDDENLY
AT HIS HOTEL

During his 14-year career with three teams in the major league, Hal
Carlson was a dependable, if not spectacular, pitcher. He broke in
with the Pittsburgh Pirates in 1917 as a 25-year-old rookie who went
7-11 as a spot starter and reliever, exhibiting a fine ERA of 2.90. He
pitched in only three games for Pittsburgh the following season due
to military service before going 8-10 in 1919.

His breakout season came in 1920 when he went 14-13, pitching in 246 innings and allowing just four home runs all season. One of the highlights of that year came when he was the starting pitcher against the St. Louis Cardinals in the first National League game held at Sportsman's Park III in St. Louis. In that contest, he bested the Cards in a 10-inning, 6-2 victory.

But the strides he had made took an unfortunate turn that off-season when the spitball was outlawed by baseball. For some reason, the Pirates failed to register him with the league as a spitball artist who could have had the use of the pitch grandfathered. As a result he was forced to stop using his "out" pitch and reinvent his repertoire on the mound.

After going 13-20 over the next three years, he was acquired by the Philadelphia Phillies where he had some of his finest seasons in the major leagues. In 1924, the 32-year-old went 8-17 for the Phillies, but seemingly was on the road to more success, finally overcoming the loss of his spitball. The 1925 season saw him rebound to a 13-14 mark in 234 innings with a league-leading four shutouts.

Carlson's best season followed in 1926 when he boasted a 17-12 record and a 3.23 ERA in a workmanlike 267 innings, with 20 complete games as a starter. He opened some eyes that season, and after getting off to a 4-5 mark for Philadelphia in 1927, the Phillies dealt him to the Chicago Cubs in exchange for Tony Kaufmann and Jimmy Cooney. The friendly confines of Wrigley Field agreed with the veteran hurler who had a 12-8 record for the Cubs for the rest of the season.

Carlson was 3-2 for Chicago the following year, appearing in just 20 games. But he rebounded for the World Series team the following year, helping the Cubs make the 1929 Fall Classic with an 11-5 record as both a spot starter and reliever. He also appeared in two games in the Series that the Cubs lost to the Philadelphia Athletics.

The 1930 season was one of high hopes for the National League defending champions and Carlson was off to a 4-2 start, one of just two Chicago hurlers with a winning record in May of that season.

But the veteran, who already was suffering from stomach ulcers, took ill during the early morning hours of May 28. On the previous evening, he had complained of stomach cramps to teammates in the lobby of the Carlos Hotel in Chicago where he rented an apartment.

At about 3 A.M., he called the team trainer complaining of severe stomach pains. Team physician Dr. John F. Davis was summoned to his room. But Hal Carlson passed away before an ambulance could arrive to take him to a hospital. Teammates Cliff Heathcote, KiKi Cuyler, and Riggs Stephenson were at Carlson's bedside when he died of a stomach hemorrhage.

ADDIE JOSS

Cleveland Indians
Pitcher

Bats: Right; Throws: Right
Height: 6 ft. 3 in.;
   Weight: 185 lbs.

Born: April 12, 1880,
   in Woodland, Wis.
Died: April 14, 1911,
   in Toledo, Ohio

Courtesy of the Baseball Hall of Fame.

Inducted into the Baseball Hall of Fame in 1978.
9 Seasons   160 Wins   97 Losses   1.89 ERA   45 Shutouts

AN OUTSTANDING PITCHER
DIES TOO YOUNG

Even at the ripe, old age of 22, Adrian "Addie" Joss could completely dominate a baseball game on the pitcher's mound. The tall right-hander led the league in shutouts with five en route to a 17-13 rookie campaign with the Cleveland Indians in 1902. In his first major league game, Joss hurled a one-hitter, surrendering only a single to Jesse Burkett, while beating the Browns, 3-0. While he wasn't quite that overpowering in the rest of his games with the Indians that year, his ERA of 2.77 was outstanding. But remarkably enough that was by far the highest ERA of his nine-year big league career.

As his career grew and his experience expanded, it seemed as though Addie Joss always gave up fewer runs over the course of a season than most of his contemporaries. His career ERA of 1.89 is second on the all-time list, right behind Ed Walsh's 1.82 mark.

After an 18-13 sophomore season with a more-than-respectable ERA of 2.19, Joss went 14-10 in 1904, yielding only 34 earned runs in nearly 200 innings for a league-leading ERA of 1.59. Incredibly, he did not allow a single home run that season.

In 1905 the tall right-hander with a wild delivery began a stretch of four consecutive 20-win seasons. He went 20-12 with an ERA of 2.01. The following season his record improved to 21-9 with a 1.72 ERA in 286 innings. That was also the year he yielded his career high in home runs with four.

Joss continued to be a workhorse on the Cleveland staff in 1907 with a league-leading 27 wins and 11 losses and a 1.83 ERA, yielding just three homers in 338 innings. As Joss's accomplishments grew on the baseball field, his personable manner made him one of the most popular players in baseball.

As a 28-year-old, he had a 24-11 record in 1908 with a league-leading 1.16 ERA. But late that season, on October 2, Joss hooked up in what might be the greatest pitching duel in the history of baseball. His Indians were fighting the White Sox and eventual pennant-winning Detroit for the league's top spot. Joss pitted against the White Sox 40-game winner Ed Walsh. All that Walsh did was strike out 15 Indians hitters, yielding just four hits and one run on the day. But that wasn't as good as the effort from Joss, who threw a no-hit, no-run perfect game, retiring 27 consecutive hitters.

The following 1909 season, 29-year-old Addie Joss had a 14-13 record with an amazing 1.71 ERA. Once again, he did not give up a single home run in 242 innings pitched. In what was to be his final season, 1910, Joss went 5-5 in just 13 games after suffering an elbow injury in Philadelphia. In spite of not being up to his usual standard of excellence, Joss boasted a 2.26 ERA and once again pitched a no-hitter against the Chicago White Sox.

Preparing for the 1911 season, it was believed that his elbow ailments were a thing of the past and that Addie Joss would once again be a dominating pitcher. But during spring training, he fainted during a game in Chattanooga. He returned home to Toledo, where he owned a pool hall and spent his off-seasons as a sports writer. He became ill at his home and died just days later of tubercular meningitis on April 14, 1911, just two days after his 31st birthday.

What Addie Joss accomplished during his nine-year major league career was remarkable. In addition to owning the second lowest ERA in the history of the game, 45 of his 160 big league wins were shutouts. The tall, slender right-hander completed 234 of 260 starts for Cleveland.

No wonder the Veterans Committee waved the 10-year minimum rule and elected Addie Joss to the Hall of Fame in 1978.

DARRYL KILE

St. Louis Cardinals
Pitcher

Bats: Right; Throws: Right
Height: 6 ft. 5 in.; Weight: 185 lbs.

Born: December 2, 1968, in Garden Grove, Calif.
Died: June 22, 2002, in Chicago, Ill.

Traded by the Colorado Rockies with Luther Hickman and
Dave Veres to the St. Louis Cardinals for Manuel Aybar,
Brent Butler, Rich Croughore, and Jose Jimenez on
November 16, 1999.
12 Seasons   133 Wins   119 Losses   4.12 ERA   9 Shutouts

A DEATH THAT ROCKED
THE BASEBALL WORLD

When he was acquired by the St. Louis Cardinals in a seven-player
trade with the Colorado Rockies in the winter of 1999, Darryl Kile
was the top of the rotation workhorse the Cards were looking for.
Kile had enjoyed good success in his tenure with the Houston Astros
and not so much success in his two seasons in Colorado.

Because of his work ethic and even-tempered demeanor, he
quickly became not just the ace of the Cardinals staff, but also one of
the most popular and dependable players on the team. His sudden

and stunning death of a massive heart attack at the age of 33 completely shocked the St. Louis organization and the entire baseball world. Not only was Kile an outstanding major league pitcher, but he was also one of the really good guys in the game.

It was an emotion-filled week as Kile pitched his club into first place in his final start on Tuesday, the same day the organization learned of the death, following a long illness, of legendary Cards broadcaster Jack Buck at the age of 77.

On Friday night, the pitcher went to dinner in Chicago with his brother Dan and some friends. By all accounts it was an early night as he returned to his suite at the Westin Hotel on Michigan Avenue around 10 P.M. In 1993, Kile's father died of a heart attack at the age of 44, but just that spring Kile passed his routine physical examination, including an EKG.

As the team prepared to take on the Chicago Cubs in an afternoon tilt at Wrigley Field, his teammates began to grow concerned when Kile did not arrive at the ballpark by 11 A.M. Repeated calls to his hotel room went unanswered and security was asked to make sure he was all right. The "Do Not Disturb" sign was hanging from the door of the 11th floor suite, and the security lock had been set from the inside of the room, making the hotel's engineering staff force their way into the room.

Darryl Kile was dead in his bed. There were no signs of foul play and the pitcher apparently did not even attempt to use his phone to call for help, evidently dying in his sleep.

An autopsy revealed that he died of a massive heart attack caused by severe coronary atherosclerosis, which caused a significant blockage of the arteries that supply blood to the heart. In fact, two of the three arteries were 90 percent blocked.

The shock and sorrow reached throughout baseball and transcended team loyalties and geographical considerations. The game had lost one of its best people.

"Darryl was a very sensitive guy," said former major league pitcher Larry Dierker, who managed Kile with Houston in 1997. "He wasn't one of those rabble-rousing athletes. He was a guy who would sit on the plane and read books while everyone else was playing poker.

"Darryl was one of the most popular guys on the team because he had the personality of a servant, living the Christian lifestyle. He'd take the blame if something went wrong and pass the credit around when something went right. He was just an ideal teammate who was very well liked.

"His death bothered our players in an enormous way. It sent shockwaves throughout the clubhouse."

The impact Darryl Kile had on the game of baseball could not have been predicted when he broke into the game as the 30th round draft choice of the Houston Astros in the 1987 amateur draft. He began his professional career in 1988 with the Astros Rookie Gulf Coast League team. In 12 starts, he had a 5-3 record, sporting a fine 3.17 ERA. In 59.2 innings, he fanned 54 hitters while walking 33.

His fine rookie campaign earned Kile a promotion to the Astros Double A farm club Columbus, in the Southern League, where he really began to open some eyes in the organization. Using a blazing fastball, Kile went 11-6 in 1989 with 108 strikeouts and 68 walks in 125.2 innings. Even though he was just 20 years old and in only his second year of professional baseball, he finished the season with AAA Tucson. In six games, he had a 2-1 record with a high ERA of 5.96. But Kile was making a case as one of the top pitching prospects in the Astros system.

After spending the 1990 season in Tucson with a 5-10 record, the following year Kile got his first taste of the major leagues. In his rookie season in the major leagues, he had a 7-11 record with a very respectable 3.69 ERA. He had a bit of a control problem, issuing 84 free passes while striking out 100 in 153.2 innings. But he gained invaluable experience that year.

He split the 1992 season between Tucson and Houston. In Triple A, he went 4-1 with a 3.99 ERA. With Houston, he had a 5-10 mark, but had a 3.95 ERA, meaning he was keeping his team in games, giving them a chance to win.

In 1993, Kile came of age and began to win. The 24-year-old went 15-8 with a 3.51 ERA. He also threw strikes, fanning 141 batters while walking just 69 in 171.2 innings. As a crowning jewel to the season, on September 8 he pitched a no-hitter against the New York Mets, winning 7-1.

Over the next seasons he had his ups and downs. He had a solid 12-11 year in 1996, followed by a 19-7 mark in 1997, pitching for Larry Dierker, who had a front row seat to enjoy the maturation of Kile as a pitcher.

"At the end, he was a really different type of pitcher than when he first started," Dierker said. "He was a real hard thrower in the minor leagues, which sort of helped to propel him to the majors. He had a great fastball and a good curve that he couldn't control. But as he matured he learned how to control the curveball which forced the batters to swing at it. Even though he didn't throw his fastball as hard as he once did, his curveball made his fastball look faster."

As an accomplished, experienced starting pitcher and still plenty of youth on his side, Kile was sought after in the free agent market following the 1997 season. Coming off a 19-win season, teams lined up to woo the big right-hander. Colorado, San Diego, Texas, and Baltimore made offers for his services but the Rockies and the Astros were the top competitors. While Houston's offer was close, the Rockies won the Darryl Kile sweepstakes with an $8 million-a-year, three-year contract. After spending his entire career with the Houston organization, Kile headed to the Mile High City.

"I don't know why he went to Colorado," said Larry Dierker. "The amazing thing to me is that pitchers ignore the empirical evidence of what other pitchers go through in a mile high altitude. Only Pedro Astascio had some real success out there. The odds are very much against you.

"That's when I got a little cynical about agents. The agent should be looking out for the best interest of the player. History tells you that pitchers don't do well out there. But if your guy signs for more money, you as the agent earn more money.

"I've learned to be philosophical about it. I know that free agency sometimes means more than who your friends are and where you want to raise your family. I was upset when he signed with Colorado, but at the same time, I understood. There are things just beyond your control. But there was only a million or so dollars difference in our offer to him over the length of the contract."

What a difference a year makes and, apparently, the light air in Colorado. Coming off his finest big league season, in 1998 Kile fell to a 13-17 mark with a 5.20 ERA. He led the National League in losses and gave up 28 home runs in 230 innings. His previous high in gopher balls surrendered was 19. The entire season was a mess for the Rockies who had their first losing season in four years, with a 77-85 record, which got Manager Don Baylor fired at season's end.

It was much of the same in 1999 as Kile once again had a losing season with the Rockies, going 8-13 with a 6.61 ERA. He also gave up a new career high in home runs with 33. Needless to say, the Colorado experiment had not gone well, and Darryl Kile's name was added to the seemingly endless number of pitchers who had difficulty in the Mile High City.

On November 16, Kile was dealt to the St. Louis Cardinals with pitchers Luther Hickman and Dave Veres in exchange for Manuel Aybar, Brent Butler, Rich Croushore, and Jose Jimenez.

Again—and what can be said on a much happier note for Darryl Kile—what a difference a year makes. Out of the high altitude and back in a normal pitching environment, Kile responded with his best year as a pro, sporting a 20-9 record with a 3.91 ERA. It was quite a turnaround after two years in Colorado that were totally out of character for a quality pitcher. St. Louis qualified for the playoffs and defeated the Atlanta Braves, three games to none, in the Divisional Playoff, and Kile won a game in that series. But the Cards were upended, four games to one, by the New York Mets in the NLCS. Kile suffered two of those losses. Even though the postseason ended in disappointment, there was little doubt that Darryl Kile was back.

He had another fine season in St. Louis in 2001 with a 16-11 record with a 3.09 ERA. He eclipsed the 200-inning plateau for the fifth time in his career and yielded just 22 home runs. The Cardinals once again advanced to postseason play, losing in the Divisional Playoffs to the eventual World Series Champion Arizona Diamondbacks. Kile pitched in one game to no decision.

The 2002 campaign was one of high hopes for St. Louis. Now 33 years old, Darryl Kile headed up a stellar pitching staff. Toward the end of June he had a 5-4 record with a 3.72 ERA in 14 starts.

And then St. Louis traveled to Chicago to take on the Cubs in the weekend series. Kile died unexpectedly, changing everything for his family and his team.

ROY MEEKER

Cincinnati Reds
Pitcher

Bats: Left; Throws: Left
Height: 5 ft. 9 in.; Weight: 175 lbs.

Born: September 15, 1900, in Lead Mine, Mo.
Died: March 25, 1929, in Orlando, Fla.

3 Years   8 Wins   14 Losses   4.73 ERA   1 Shutout

DIED WHILE PURSUING
HIS BIG LEAGUE DREAMS

The career of diminutive southpaw Roy Meeker, much like his life, was much too short, leaving more questions than answers. Born in Lead Mine, Mo., Meeker made his home in Kansas City, Kans., but spent his summers pursuing his major league dream.

In his first big league action, the 22-year-old broke in with the 1923 Philadelphia Athletics, serving notice that he would make a serious run for a regular spot on the pitching staff. He pitched in five games with an impressive 3-0 record and an acceptable 3.60 ERA, especially eye-opening for a young pitcher. In addition, Meeker completed both games he started for Connie Mack's nine.

The next year, in 1924, Meeker made the A's roster and pitched in 30 games. But his second-season stats were not nearly as impressive. He went 5-12 with a 4.68 ERA, starting 14 games, completing five of them with one shutout. But in 146 innings he surrendered 166 hits. The little lefty's major problem was control, as he issues 81 free passes while striking out just 37 batters that year.

Roy Meeker spent the entire 1925 season, and most of the following season, in the minor leagues, pitching in Portland and Columbus, the Cincinnati Reds American Association affiliate. Later in the 1926 season, he was back in the major leagues and appeared in seven games for the Reds, going 0-2, with a high ERA of 6.43. He gave up 24 hits in 21 innings, but again walked nine batters while fanning only five.

He spent the next two years pitching in the minor leagues trying to get another shot at the major leagues. On March 25, 1929, while working out with the Reds in spring training, at Orlando, Meeker complained of not feeling well after a morning workout. He returned to his room at about noon and died shortly thereafter of a heart attack.

URBAN
SHOCKER

Courtesy of the Baseball Hall of Fame.

New York Yankees
Pitcher

Bats: Right; Throws: Right
Height: 5 ft. 10 in.;
   Weight: 170 lbs.

Born: August 22, 1890,
   in Cleveland, Ohio
Died: September 9, 1928,
   in Denver, Colo.

Acquired by the New York Yankees from the St. Louis
   Browns for Joe Bush, Milt Gaston, and Joe Girard on
   December 17, 1924.
13 Seasons   187 Wins   117 Losses   3.17 ERA

TOP HURLER TOUGH
ON THE YANKEES

In his 17 seasons as a big league manager, Miller Huggins developed
a reputation as being a very knowledgeable baseball man with a keen
feel for the game. His teams won 1,413 games in his career, and in
12 years at the helm of the New York Yankees, the Bronx Bombers finished in first place six times and second two times. But when it came
to a pitcher named Urban Shocker, Miller Huggins had it all wrong.

Formerly a catcher, Shocker was converted to a pitcher in his first professional season of 1913 because of his good velocity and accuracy. As he learned his new trade, the right-hander developed a good spitball and a variety of breaking pitches thrown at different speeds. After a year with the Windsor Club of the Border League, Shocker spent two seasons with Ottawa of the Canadian League, winning 20 games in 1914. He was then purchased by the New York Yankees, managed by "Wild Bill" Donovan.

Shocker went 4-3 for the Yanks in 1916, appearing in 12 games and sporting a 2.62 ERA. The following season he went 8-5 in 26 games, yielding just 124 hits in 145 innings with a 2.61 ERA.

But at the end of the 1917 season Donovan was replaced by Huggins, who then dispatched Shocker along with Nick Cullop, Joe Gedeon, Fritz Maisel, Les Nunamaker, and $15,000 to the St. Louis Browns in exchange for Eddie Plank and Del Pratt.

To say that the deal backfired is an understatement as Plank never reported to the Yankees, and Urban Shocker, while a member of the Browns, developed into one of the best pitchers in baseball. In fairness to the Yankees skipper, second baseman Pratt had three good seasons in New York, solving a major problem for the Yankees. But the player who enjoyed the most success following the trade was none other than Urban Shocker. Take that, Miller Huggins.

After his first year in St. Louis, in which he went 6-5 in just 14 games, Shocker began to come in to his own in 1919, with a 13-11 record and a 2.60 ERA in 30 games. In 1920, Shocker began a four-year string of 20-win seasons, going 20-10 in 38 games. He had his career high in wins in 1921 with a 27-12 mark, while eating up 326 innings along the way. His workmanlike efforts continued in 1922 when the 31-year-old pitched 348 innings en route to a 24-17 mark.

Shocker had his final 20-win season in 1923 with a 20-12 record, but a disagreement with Browns' management at the end of the season led the way for his eventual return to New York.

Shocker was fined and suspended by the St. Louis after he failed to make the last East Coast road trip with the team. The pitcher was upset that the club would not allow him to bring his wife along. In those days, bringing the Mrs. along on a road trip was not accepted behavior. Shocker hired an attorney and attempted to have Baseball Commissioner Kenesaw Mountain Landis grant him free agency. He eventually dropped his appeal and even received a $3,000 raise in salary to return to the Browns for the 1924 season.

New Browns manager George Sisler and Shocker were old friends and former teammates and management allowed Sisler to keep his friend on the team. Shocker didn't let Sisler down as he responded with a respectable 16-13 season in which he threw 246 innings.

During his years in St. Louis, Urban Shocker had become known as the "Nemesis of the Yankees," beating the Bronx Bombers 20 times, even though he lost 21 games to them. But over the years, Miller Huggins grew to admire his guts on the pitcher's mound and respected his pitching ability, which led to a deal that saw Shocker return to the Yankees in December 1924 in a trade with St. Louis receiver Joe Bush, Milt Gaston, and Joe Girard.

The right-hander was not the big winner that the Yankees had hoped, but at the age of 34, he still ate up 244 innings with a respectable 12-12 record. Shocker was one of the pitchers whose use of the spitball was grandfathered as a legal pitch for him after it was banned by baseball in 1920.

The following season, Shocker rebounded nicely with a 19-11 record, followed by another respectable 18-6 mark in 1927. Even as he grew older, in spite of the fact that Shocker was allowed to throw the spitball, he threw the fastball and curve most often. The wily old veteran often used the threat of the spitball to confuse hitters at the plate.

At the end of the 1927 season, he announced his retirement, feeling he was ready to devote his time to his other career as a radio salesman. Shocker said he also planned to get his pilot's license. But the pitcher's health had also become a concern as he suffered from mitral valve failure. For a number of years, he had not been able to fall asleep while laying down and had to sit up in order to do so.

The Yankees and he agreed that he would play one more season in 1928, but he appeared in just one game in May and was let go by the club in July. Health concerns took Shocker to Denver that summer where he pitched in a semi-pro game, possibly with the idea of making one more run at the major leagues. But a bout with pneumonia and his existing heart condition saw him hospitalized in August of that year in Denver.

While he appeared to be on the road to recovery, Urban Shocker took a turn for the worst and died on September 9, 1928, at the age of 38. Although he has never received serious consideration for the Baseball Hall of Fame, while seven of his teammates on the 1927 Yankees have been inducted, Urban Shocker was one of the top pitchers in baseball during most of the 1920s.

DANNY THOMPSON

Courtesy of the Minnesota Twins.

Texas Rangers
Infielder

Bats: Right; Throws: Right
Height: 6 ft.;
    Weight: 183 lbs.

Born: February 1, 1947,
    in Wichita, Kans.
Died: December 10, 1972,
    in Rochester, Minn.

Drafted by the Minnesota Twins in the first round of the 1968
    amateur draft.
7 Seasons   .248 BA   15 HR   194 RBIs

AN AMERICAN DREAM
CUT SHORT

Former Minnesota Twins and Texas Rangers shortstop Danny
Thompson lived just about every American boy's dream. He was a
major league baseball player who married his high school sweetheart
and had a beautiful young family. The sky was the limit for this All-
American at Oklahoma State University, or so it seemed.

But just prior to his fourth major league season with the Minnesota Twins, on January 31, 1973, Thompson learned that he had leukemia during what had begun as a typically routine physical examination.

"Like all the other Twins that lived year-round in the Twin Cities, he went to the team physician for a routine physical before heading south for spring training," said Jo Thompson, Danny's widow. "The lab called the next day asking him to come back for a blood test because of some problem with the first test. After the second test, the team physician asked him to go to the University of Minnesota Hospitals for a bone marrow biopsy, which he did. I majored in medical technology as an undergraduate and I knew exactly what they were looking for. When he asked, I told him that bone marrow biopsies were sometimes done to test for leukemia. He looked at me as if I was crazy.

"A few days later he was given the bad news and referred to a hematologist at the Mayo Clinic. Initially, he was able to manage the illness through oral medication that brought his white blood cell count down."

Thompson had learned he was suffering from chronic granulocytic leukemia, a pretty miserable 26th birthday present. Following the 1974 season, he underwent the experimental series of injections meant to combat the progression of the killer disease and was able to play baseball throughout the process. He received six shots the first year and two shots per year after that. But the treatment was painful and left him with half dollar–sized scars on his skin.

"He also went through a trial procedure in which leukemia cells from another person were injected into his arm, like smallpox vaccinations," said Jo Thompson. "All that did was to create huge scabs that ultimately fell off leaving his arms with multiple scars."

Thompson was a likeable guy and a hard-nosed ballplayer. He was a friend to both young players and veterans in Minnesota.

"Danny and I became good friends when he was playing with the Twins and continued after he was traded to Texas," said Minnesota

Twins Hall of Famer Harmon Killebrew, who slugged 573 home runs in his 22-year major league career. "He was a fine young man. His school was so small that his high school graduation class had just four people in it. They were all boys. He used to joke about the graduation dance. I've got so many fond memories of Danny. After the games we'd go out and just talk about baseball and talk about hitting. Players don't do that so much these days."

A native of Wichita, Kans., he was a multiple-sport star at Capron High School, where he met his wife, Jo, following one of his basketball games. He attended Oklahoma State and caught the eye of professional scouts. He was drafted by the Yankees, Reds, and Senators but chose not to sign. Finally, when he was picked in the first round of the amateur draft, secondary phase, by the Minnesota Twins in June 1968, he signed on the dotted line and became a professional baseball player.

Thompson was assigned to St. Cloud of the Northern League where the 21-year-old hit .282 in 63 games. He quickly worked his way up through the Twins farm system earning a promotion to Double A Charlotte of the Southern League for his first full season as a professional. He responded well, hitting .302.

In 1970, his final minor league season, Thompson was in Evansville of the American Association, Minnesota's Triple A farm club. The shortstop was hitting .247 before being recalled to the big club, where he got his first taste of The Show. While he hit just .219 in 96 games for the Twins, the club was impressed with its young infielder. He also had a hit-and-walk in their playoff series against Baltimore, which the Orioles won three games to none. But Danny Thompson was a big leaguer.

"Danny was good enough to play in the majors," said his wife Jo. "That's a superlative achievement considering that in 1970 he was one of only 600 to 700 combined major league jobs. However, he was never a star in the sense that Harmon Killebrew, Rod Carew, Jim Perry, and Tony Oliva were. It looked to both of us that the future was limitless and he was about as happy as a person could have been.

"Danny was old school when it came to baseball. He didn't play for the money. The most he ever made in his professional career was $37,000. I think he would have played for free. He played because he loved the game.

"On many occasions, I heard him talk with some degree of anxiety about what his life would be [like] when he could no longer play in the majors. For that reason, he wanted to be a college baseball coach so that he could stay close to the game. In the weeks before he died in December 1976, his consuming thought was to recover enough to go to spring training."

Thompson's first full season in the majors in 1971 was interrupted by an arm injury that limited him to just 48 games in which he hit .263. The frustration of his rookie season was lightened as in 1972 a healthy Danny Thompson played in his career high of 144 games and hit a solid .276 with four homers and another career best 48 RBIs. The likeable shortstop had arrived as a major league player.

"He was a better than average player," commented Killebrew. "Danny was a good fielding shortstop who was also a pretty good hitter. He wasn't a power hitter, he was more of a line drive hitter. Then they found that he had the disease during his routine physical."

It was that winter that Thompson discovered he had leukemia. But his disease was not enough to keep him away from the game he loved so dearly. It was originally felt that the disease was controllable. In 1973, though often sick, he played in 99 games and hit .225. In 1974, his average improved to .250. That off-season, he began the experimental drug injections at the Mayo Clinic.

"He'd come in to the clubhouse with these dots the size of dollar bills on his arms," said Killebrew. "To talk to him, you'd never know there was anything wrong with him. He just went about his business, like there was nothing wrong. Sometimes he'd come in after a treatment and you knew he had a hard time. But he never complained, or felt sorry for himself."

Danny Thompson was the winner of the Hutch Award that winter, named for former major league pitcher and manager Fred

Hutchinson, who died of cancer on November 12, 1964. The award is given each year to the major league player "who best exemplifies the fighting spirit and competition displayed by the late Fred Hutchinson."

He responded well on the playing field having his best season for the 1975 Twins since the discovery of the disease. Thompson played in 112 games and hit .270 at a career high of five home runs and 37 RBIs. On the field, he appeared to be on his way back to where he was before learning of the leukemia.

But in 1976 Thompson slumped, hitting just .234 in 34 games for the Twins. On June 1, he and pitcher Bert Blyleven were traded by Minnesota to the Texas Rangers in exchange for Bill Singer, Roy Smalley, Mike Cubbage, Jim Gideon, and $250,000. The blockbuster deal saw Thompson relegated to a utility role with the Rangers. He finished the season in Texas, hitting .214 in 64 games. Shockingly, just two months after the conclusion of the season, Danny Thompson was dead.

After a valiant fight, Thompson lost his life on December 10, 1976, at St. Mary's Hospital in Rochester, Minn., at the age of 29. Not all that many years before, the future of Danny Thompson seemed to be bright.

"During the last six months of his life, the oral medication became less and less effective," said Jo Thompson. "It ultimately failed altogether. By that time the leukemia had changed from the chronic phase to the acute phase and the docs were really unable to do much for him. His attitude about the illness was that he would beat it. He remained upbeat about it until the very end. Part of that optimism was due to his strong religious faith. The other part of it was due to a young man's sense of immortality and the power of denial.

"I really believe that Danny couldn't acknowledge that he would die of his illness before he reached the age of 30. He was typical of many men that feel that to acknowledge a devastating fact is to give in to it. I don't know if there was any real contemplation of death in his heart of hearts. If there was, he never spoke of it to me directly.

However, during the last year of his life, he indirectly indicated that he may have known he wouldn't make it. Once he jokingly told me that he'd purchased enough life insurance before the diagnosis to leave me a rich widow.

"During his final days, he poignantly told me that he wished he could live to see our daughters grow up and marry. I was a basket case during those years. I knew the type of leukemia he had was even more deadly than children's leukemia and that there was virtually no chance of long-term recovery. I knew that I was going to have to raise our children by myself and felt angry, frightened, and most of all, profoundly sad. I wish that I had been able to manage my own grief so that I could have helped him mourn for the impending end of his life."

Danny Thompson led a full, if short, life. But the few years he had in major league baseball made their mark. He has not been forgotten and his name will always be known for the heroism he showed fighting his fatal disease.

"After that season in 1976, he went to the Mayo Clinic and he died there," said Killebrew. "I went to his funeral in Oklahoma and was so touched by Danny and his life and the person he was. I thought that while there was nothing I could do for Danny, maybe we could help the situation for other people."

Killebrew, a native of Payette, Idaho, approached former legislator Ralph Harding about starting a golf tournament to raise funds to fight the disease that killed his friend at the age of 29.

In 1977 the first Danny Thompson Memorial Golf Tournament was held in Sun Valley, Idaho. The event, known as the "Tournament with a Heart," has become a living tribute to Danny Thompson, the person for whom it was named. To date, the tournament has raised more than $86.1 million for research for the University of Minnesota Leukemia Research Foundation and Mountain States Tumor Institute of Boise.

With the passage of time, Danny Thompson's family often wonders where life would have taken them had he lived.

"I remember Danny as a good man, capable of love and friendship, who faced his illness with courage and dignity," said Jo Thompson. "I often wonder how he would have aged with the passage of time. I know how much I have changed and wonder if we would have walked down the same path over the years. I know that my daughters have expressed some of the same questions and fantasies about him, as they think about knowing him as adults, as if he had lived."

Jo Thompson is director of operations at SGA Youth & Family Services in Chicago. Her daughter Tracy, 35, is a financial analyst for Washington Hospital Center. Another daughter, Dana, 32, works in the publishing industry.

Tracy Mickle was just six years old when her father died. She was old enough to have memories of her father, but has always yearned for more.

"I often wonder how our lives would have been different had he lived," said Tracy. "My mother becoming a single parent and raising two kids was really unexpected. He never really thought that he was going to die from leukemia and they were both very unprepared for what was to come. If he were alive, even after he retired, he would have been involved in the game he loved so much as a coach, or some other area.

"I do think of him quite often, especially when life's milestones occur, like when I got married, or graduated from college and grad school. At such sentimental times I think of how proud he would have been. I was such a daddy's little girl. I always think about what life with him as an adult would be."

JIM UMBRICHT

....

Houston Colt .45s
Pitcher

Bats: Right; Throws: Right
Height: 6 ft. 4 in.; Weight: 215 lbs.

Born: September 17, 1930, in Chicago, Ill.
Died: April 8, 1964, in Houston, Tex.

Drafted by the Houston Colt .45s from the Pittsburgh Pirates
    in the 1961 expansion draft.
5 Seasons   9 Wins   5 Losses   3 Saves   3.06 ERA

A COURAGEOUS ATHLETE

While not many of today's baseball fans know who Big Jim Umbricht
was, just about every fan of the game has seen pictures of the headstone of the Houston Colt .45s pitcher, who passed away in April
1964 at the age of 33. His headstone is nothing less than the Houston
Astrodome.

"After he died, we flew over the big hole in the ground that
became the Astrodome and I spread his ashes there," said his brother
Ed Umbricht. "So the Houston Astrodome is Jim's headstone."

In addition, the Houston franchise honored its fallen friend and
made Umbricht's No. 32 the first number retired by the team to ensure
it would never be worn by another Astro player. Not too shabby for

a journeyman pitcher with a 9-5 big league record spread over five seasons. But Jim Umbricht always brought more to the game than what was simply expressed in the box score.

Before the big leagues expanded in 1962, there were only 16 major league cities for players to realize their professional dreams. As a result, hundreds of players never had a chance to show whether or not they had the right stuff for The Show. Unlike today's game, where the quality of play has been diluted with so many teams giving much less talented players big league careers, only the cream of the crop got to play major league baseball during this golden era.

"He was a pretty good relief pitcher," said Umbricht's teammate, pitcher Ken Johnson, a 13-year big league veteran who was the ace of the Houston Colt .45s' staff. "He was the guy who came into the game and put out the fire. Jim had the fastball, curve, slider, and change up. But he was a real bulldog who would go get you.

"You couldn't find a nicer guy. We were roommates and he was like a brother to me. He always took care of me. We both liked to play cards a lot and Jim was a smart gambler, much better than I was. He always gave me the sign that it was time to get out."

A native of Chicago, Ill., it took Umbricht eight minor league seasons to make it to the major leagues. After earning his degree at the University of Georgia, where he played both baseball and basketball, he broke into professional baseball with Waycross of the Georgia-Florida League in 1953 with a 4-3 record and an impressive 2.87 ERA. The only pitching the big right-hander did in 1954 and '55 was as a member of the U.S. Army, pitching for Fort Carson, Colo. He made quite an impression there as he fanned 17 batters in the army championship game of 1955.

Following his military stint, Umbricht continued his pro career in 1956 with Baton Rouge of the Evangeline League. The workhorse went 15-15, leading the league with 27 complete games and 235 innings pitched. That earned him a promotion to Topeka of the Western League in 1957 where he went 13-8. After a subpar 6-10 campaign with Atlanta of the Southern Association in 1958, Umbricht rebounded nicely with an outstanding 14-8 year the following season with a stellar 2.78 ERA in 136 innings. That prompted his call-up to the parent club, the Pittsburgh Pirates, in 1959. In his only action, Umbricht pitched seven innings to no decision.

Jim Umbricht was one of many players trying to make the jump from the minor leagues to the majors with the Pittsburgh Pirates organization. In the World Championship season of 1960, Umbricht split the season between Columbus of the International League where he went 8-5 in 19 games and the Pirates, where he had a 1-2 mark in 17 games. He was not on the postseason roster.

With quality pitching enough to win a World Championship in 1960, the Bucs were a tough pitching staff to make, even for a top-notch prospect like Umbricht. Having had the chance to pitch in 17 games with the Pirates during that season, Umbricht finally seemed to be getting his opportunity. But the Pittsburgh staff always had more good pitchers than available spots, so he spent most of 1961 at Columbus, with a 9-6 record, while pitching in just one game with the Pirates.

Those brief stints in the Steel City with the Pirates as well as having outstanding minor league credentials helped him become one of the players chosen by the Houston Colt .45s in the expansion draft for the 1962 season. Houston general manager Paul Richards had been familiar with Umbricht ever since Big Jim paid his way to a Milwaukee Braves tryout camp in Waycross in 1953.

"He worked very, very hard to become a major leaguer, going from the lowest level to the top," said Ed Umbricht of his brother. "He just accepted the trips back and forth to the minors as a way of life. But come Hell or high water, he was going to be a major league player. He worked at it from day one. From the time he was 10 years old he knew that's what he wanted. I can still remember him practicing sliding in the field next to our house when he was just a kid because he knew he'd have to be able to do that when he became a major league player."

After three different trips from the minors to the majors and back again with the Pirates, Umbricht made the opening-day roster of the

Colt .45s and pitched well. But fate played a nasty trick on him as he was optioned to Triple A Oklahoma City in May because he was caught up in a numbers game once again. When Houston acquired veteran hurler Don McMahon from Milwaukee, Umbricht was the only pitcher who could be optioned to the minors to make room. Rather than mope at yet another stint in the minors, he pitched well in Oklahoma City and was back in the bigs in July after 23 games.

Once he got back to the parent club he showed them what they were missing and responded by being the only undefeated pitcher on the staff with a 4-0 record and a miserly 2.01 ERA. After years of waiting for his big chance, Jim Umbricht had his first extended opportunity in the major leagues, pitching in 34 games. His first three chances with Pittsburgh saw him appear in a total of just 19 games. He had finally made it and his future seemed bright.

At the height of his major league baseball career, Jim Umbricht was one of the most effective pitchers on the Houston Colt .45s' staff. In his ninth professional season, after turning pro with the Waycross farm club in the Milwaukee organization in 1953, he finally was pitching in major leagues and had made his mark as a dependable member of the staff.

It took expansion to give Umbricht his real chance that finally came with the Colt .45s, a team in desperate need of pitching. His tough attitude and makeup had caught the eye of Paul Richards all those years before. In fact, the GM and the big right-hander developed a friendship that resulted in the two playing golf together every day during spring training in 1963.

It was during one of their golf outings that Umbricht confided that a small lump had appeared on his leg. After looking at the growth, Richards insisted that Umbricht travel back to Houston immediately to have it looked at by medical professionals. He checked into the M. D. Anderson Cancer Clinic and was told that he had lymphoma, which had spread to his leg, thigh, and groin. On March 8, Umbricht underwent more than six hours of surgery at Methodist Hospital in Houston to remove the cancerous tumors.

Two months later, he was back on the mound pitching for the Houston Colt .45s with more than 100 stitches in his leg.

"After he had the surgery, we all thought that he was going to be all right," said Ken Johnson. "He thought so too. He was such a competitor. During games when he was pitching, blood would start to come through his uniform, from where he had the surgery and the stitches were. He'd have to go in to the clubhouse and put on a new bandage to keep the blood from showing through his uniform. He would just never quit."

While the initial prognosis after surgery was encouraging, Umbricht soon learned that he was dying.

"He came back after the surgery and pitched for the rest of the season," said Ed Umbricht. "He thought he was cured. But when he came back pitching, he was really hurting. No matter what, he was giving it his all. He wanted to be able to continue, but God simply wouldn't let him do it because it was his time to go. The doctors were very frank with him and the family."

In spite of his bleak outlook, Umbricht pitched well with a 4-3 record in 35 games with a 2.61 ERA. In fact, he yielded just 52 hits in 72 innings. But few knew of the courage he showed every day as he made his comeback and pitched effectively in spite of the ominous prognosis.

That winter he was named "Most Courageous Athlete" by the Philadelphia sportswriters. At the dinner at which he was honored, he lit up a cigar following the meal. When asked why he would smoke a cigar, he quipped, "Well, they tell me that cigarette smoking causes cancer."

But that November he was back in the hospital and learned that the rapidly spreading melanoma was incurable. Although he had a burning desire to live until the opening day of the 1964 baseball season, Umbricht passed away on April 8, five days before the Colts opening game against the Cincinnati Reds. In that game, his roommate, Ken Johnson, opposed Jim Maloney, and the ace of the staff dedicated the game to his fallen comrade.

"He was more than a brother to me, he was my best friend," said Ed Umbricht. "I'm very proud of him. He just accepted what happened to him. Jim was a very humble individual."

The team's much-liked member's uniform number 32 was retired. Today, it hangs in the Houston Astros new stadium, Minute Maid Field. And even though the Astros now play their games in a different venue, the old Houston Astrodome, known as the Eighth Wonder of the World, remains.

It is still the head stone of Big Jim Umbricht.

RUBE WADDELL

St. Louis Browns
Pitcher

Bats: Right; Throws: Left
Height: 6 ft. 1 in.; Weight: 196 lbs.

Born: October 13, 1876, in Bradford, Pa.
Died: April 1, 1914, in San Antonio, Tex.

Purchased by the St. Louis Browns from the Philadelphia
Athletics on February 7, 1908. Inducted into the Baseball
Hall of Fame by the Veterans Committee in 1946.
13 Seasons   193 Wins   143 Losses   2.16 ERA

A TALENTED AND FASCINATING
CHARACTER OF THE GAME

What would you get if you crossed Sandy Koufax, Steve Carlton, Nolan Ryan, and Wilber Wood with Jimmy Piersall, Mark Fidrych, Richie Allen, Steve Howe, and Grover Cleveland Alexander? Odds are that such a combination might begin to describe the many sides of the great left-handed pitcher Rube Waddell.

It has often been said that you need to have a lot of little boy in you to be a major league baseball player. George Edward "Rube" Waddell left no doubt that he had more little boy inside of him than anything else during his Hall of Fame career, with the possible exception of his incredible ability on the pitcher's mound.

His life was the stuff of legend. On the field his accomplishments are well documented and amazingly impressive. His antics off the playing field are also the stuff of legend, but not nearly as easy to trace. Are the stories about him truth, fiction, or an enhanced combination of the two?

When he wasn't befuddling opposing batters with his outstanding fastball, nearly unhittable curve, and pinpoint control, Rube Waddell was also preoccupied with his many other interests. Life was a candy store in which Waddell tasted many different flavors. In fact, during his life he had more jobs than a cat has lives and more interests than a grand jury in a crooked town. With apologies to the folks at Saturday Night Live and their Wild and Crazy Guys, that mold was broken with the appearance of Rube Waddell.

Not only was he a Hall of Fame pitcher, but he was also an alligator wrestler, a fishing fanatic, a marbles enthusiast, a drunk, a bartender, a rugby player, and a legitimate hero whose efforts actually saved lives. While he has been labeled by many as a simple-minded, country bumpkin, and a hick, it seems much more fair to consider that Waddell may well have had the most extreme case of attention deficit disorder that major league baseball has ever seen.

A particularly intense game of marbles would often be the cause of Waddell's tardiness for a baseball game. He would supposedly arrive at the ballpark in street clothes and change into his uniform while running across the field to the clubhouse, a particularly entertaining habit since he allegedly wore no underwear. Legend also has it that the lefty would run off of the pitcher's mound during a game to chase a fire engine that had its siren wailing.

His incredible talent on the playing field coupled with an endearing simplicity made him a favorite of the fans everywhere he played. A member of Connie Mack's Philadelphia Athletics for six years, Waddell was the toast of the City of Brotherly Love, spending hours playing ball with kids on the street, tending bar at local watering holes, and becoming a regular at fire stations.

At one point Waddell saved the lives of two men on a hunting trip who were drowning. He also was credited for his quick thinking in a crowded department store. He picked up a blazing oil stove and removed it from the store before a fire broke out.

While his off-the-field antics and on-the-field eccentricities are interesting and entertaining, Rube Waddell's talent as a major league pitcher was just about as good as it gets. In his 13-year career, he won 193 games with a brilliant 2.16 ERA. He ranks 42nd all time in career strikeouts with 2,316, ahead of pitchers such as Juan Marichal (2,303), Lefty Grove (2,266), Eddie Plank (2,246), Jim Palmer (2,212), and Grover Cleveland Alexander (2,198). His single season mark of 349 strikeouts in 1904 ranks as the 18th best of all time. But narrowing it down to the 20th century, he ranks second among left-handed pitchers, behind only Sandy Koufax, who fanned 382 in 1965.

On July 1, 1902, Rube Waddell became the first pitcher in major league history to strike out the side on just nine pitches. Three years later, in 1905, he was the first hurler to win the triple crown—most wins with 27, most strikeouts with 287, and the lowest ERA at 1.48. His former manager Connie Mack called him the greatest pitcher, in terms of raw talent, that he had ever seen. But any discussion about this talented southpaw always includes his behavior and background. For it was also Mack who reportedly said that Waddell had a $2 million body and a two cent head.

Rube was born in the middle of farm country in Bradford, Pa., in 1876. Just 18 years later, he was pitching for a minor league team in Butler, Pa., and another in Detroit. Even at that early age, his penchant for drinking and rowdy behavior made his presence on a team of questionable value. But the entertainment value was not to be ignored.

Once a teammate observed him soaking his pitching arm in ice and inquired as to why he was doing so. Waddell said he was afraid he would burn the catcher's glove if he didn't cool his arm off.

He broke into the major leagues with the Louisville Colonels in 1897, going 0-1 in two games. After more seasoning the following year, he returned to the team in 1899 and had a 7-2 record in 10 games.

With the league planning to consolidate and do away with certain franchises, Louisville owner Barney Dreyfuss purchased the Pittsburgh Pirates and traded some of his best players to the Steel City. To that end, on December 8, 1899, one of the biggest trades in baseball history occurred. Louisville traded Waddell along with Fred Clarke, Bert Cunningham, Mike Kelley, Tacks Latimer, Tommy Leach, Tom Messitt, Deacon Phillipe, Claude Ritchey, Jack Wadsworth, Honus Wagner, and Chief Zimmer to Pittsburgh in exchange for Jack Chesbro, Paddy Fox, John O'Brien, Art Madison, and $25,000.

After having an 8-13 record in Pittsburgh in 1900, in May 1901, with an 0-2 record, Waddell was purchased by the Chicago Orphans where he rebounded with a 14-14 record. Prior to the start of the 1902 season, he jumped from the Orphans and found a new home in Philadelphia with the A's.

Success was immediate as the 25-year-old had a 24-7 record with a 2.05 ERA in the first of four consecutive 20-win seasons. As he continued to eat up innings, with 324 in 1903, he had another fine year with a 21-16 record and a 2.44 ERA. Waddell eclipsed 300 strikeouts in a season for the first time as he garnered 302.

This was also the year that Waddell was in a vaudeville play, "The Stain of Guilt," again exhibiting a wandering mind. But he also had a quick wit, which was displayed when at one point during his career a manager told him he was being fined for a disgraceful hotel episode in Detroit. When confronted with the subject, he reportedly replied that his manager was a liar since there "ain't no Hotel Episode in Detroit."

He went 25-19 in 1904 with the amazing 349 strikeouts in 383 innings and a 1.62 ERA in 46 games. That outstanding year was a precursor to the triple crown gem of a season in 1905 when Waddell led the league with 27 wins, 287 strikeouts, and a 1.48 ERA. That season saw Rube hook up and beat Cy Young in a 20-inning game.

But because of an arm injury he sustained in a fight with a teammate on a train ride, he was unable to pitch in the World Series. The
A's lost to the Giants in the Fall Classic without their star left-handed
pitcher. Ugly rumors that were never substantiated were also present
that gamblers had paid him to miss the series.

An interesting contract negotiation occurred between Waddell
and his manager Connie Mack.

"In 1905, Waddell refused to sign his contract," wrote Max
Silberman, Philadelphia Athletics Historical Society historian. "Mr.
Mack assured him that he would not get another dime. Waddell replied
that he did not want more money, only a guarantee [that] his roommate and catcher Ossie Schreckengost (Schreck) [would] be forbidden
to eat animal crackers in bed. In those days, roommates shared a double bed and Schreck's crumbs or noise annoyed Waddell. An alternate
version of this apocryphal tale was that Waddell ate the crackers and
Schreck complained to Connie Mack. In any event, Mr. Mack had his
hands full with these two talented, but simple-minded, roommates."

Whether his arm failed to mend properly, if his lifestyle finally
caught up with him, or a combination of the two, while Rube
Waddell continued to be an effective pitcher, there seemed to be a
perceptive drop in his game. The 20-win streak was over as he went
15-17 in 1906 with a 2.21 ERA. In 272 innings, Waddell fanned 196
hitters. In 1907, he rebounded with a 19-13 season with the A's with
a 2.15 ERA. He struck out 232 batters in 284 innings.

Following that season he was purchased by the St. Louis Browns
where the 31-year-old responded with a 19-14 campaign with an
outstanding 1.89 ERA with 232 SOs. The following season in
St. Louis, he slipped to 11-14 with a 2.37 ERA and just 141 strikeouts in 220 innings.

He was 3-1 with the Browns in 1910 when the club released him.
After a brief stint in the Eastern League, Waddell resurfaced with the
Minneapolis Millers. A damn broke, and always the first person to
offer assistance, he stood in chest-high freezing water helping to stack
sandbags and caught pneumonia.

Never fully recovered from that illness, he continued to drink heavily and was eventually sent by Minneapolis manager Joe Cantillon to a sanitarium in San Antonio, Texas, where he was treated for tuberculosis. Four months later, on April 1, 1914, April Fool's Day, Rube Waddell died at the age of 38.

One of the most brilliant baseball careers and a fascinating and interesting life had ended before its time. In another sad irony, his cracker-eating teammate with the Athletics, Ossie "Schreck" Schreckengost, died at the age of 39 just four months later.

DICK WANTZ

California Angels
Pitcher

Bats: Right; Throws: Right
Height: 6 ft. 5 in.;
    Weight: 175 lbs.

Courtesy of Angels Baseball.

Born: April 11, 1940, in South Gate, Calif.
Died: May 13, 1965, in Inglewood, Calif.

Signed as an amateur free agent by the California Angels
    in 1961.
1 Season   0 Wins   0 Losses   18.00 ERA

A SUDDEN AND UNTIMELY DEATH

Had he not chosen to become a professional baseball player, the odds
are that Dick Wantz may have had the ability to be a professional
golfer. But baseball was his first love and after three minor league seasons and a whirlwind spring training with the Angels in 1965, Wantz
pitched his way onto the big league roster.

The tall, slender, bespectacled, hard-throwing, right-handed
pitcher was highly touted in the Angels organization. Signed to a
professional contract after he went 5-1 for California State University,

Los Angeles, in 1961, Wantz impressed as he progressed through the farm system although he was not a big winner down on the farm. But his nasty sidearm delivery and heavy fastball that he threw in the low 90s made him a tough pitcher to face as he was all business on the pitcher's mound.

He won only five games for Tri-Cities and Hawaii in 1964, but had a stellar training camp to literally force his way into the last available spot on the pitching staff. Wantz made his major league debut on opening day of the season, April 13, giving up two runs and three hits in one inning. The tall right-hander did strike out two batters in his inaugural outing.

"He and I got to know each other very well," said Dr. Paul Schaal, an infielder for 11 major league seasons with the Angels and Kansas City Royals, who is now a chiropractor in Overland Park, Kans. "Dick was a tall, lanky right-hander who was a hard thrower. In my opinion, he had a major league career ahead of him. In addition to his good fastball, he also threw a good slider. On the mound he was a winner. He was the type of guy you like to play behind, but not the kind you'd like to face in the batter's box. With that nasty sidearm delivery and a hard fastball, it's kind of tough for a right-handed hitter to keep that left foot in the batter's box. Our manager Bill Rigney loved him."

But Wantz saw his seemingly bright pitching career put on hold as he began experiencing severe headaches while the Angels played an April series against the New York Yankees. When the team visited Detroit, the big hurler was hospitalized for a short while. Originally diagnosed as suffering from a blood virus, Wantz was released from the hospital and returned home to Southern California, feeling much better, hoping to pick up where he left off with his first season in the major leagues.

But that had not been his first experience with severe headaches. They were a part of his life that teammates saw years before he played with the Angels.

"Even in the minor leagues he used to get some really bad headaches," said Paul Schaal. "They became more frequent. He was taking pain pills. You didn't hear much about brain tumors in those days. There's a lot more they can do for you these days."

Wantz was again hospitalized and given a spinal tap and X-ray, which showed a brain tumor. The local-boy-made-good underwent surgery. Team physician Robert Wood stated after the operation that the tall right-hander's condition would no doubt prove fatal. The doctors apparently removed as much of the cancerous brain tissue as possible, but then discovered a bilateral cancer that had stricken both sides of the brain.

Following surgery, Wantz went into a coma and never regained consciousness.

Dick Wantz died on May 13, 1965, at Daniel Freeman Hospital, exactly one month following his lone appearance in the major leagues. More than 300 people attended his funeral, including the entire California Angles baseball team.

"You mourn and you miss your teammate," said Schaal. "Everybody liked him. Most of us just coming up to the majors were scared to death. But he had a lot of confidence. It was not a cocky attitude or anything, but he just went out there and challenged people. On the field, he was a winner.

"He was a great guy with a good personality who liked to have fun. I still think of him because we were friends. He loved his wife and their baby. What I remember most about him wasn't the ballplayer on the field. It was the laughing. He was so much fun in the clubhouse, always clowning around. He was a friend of everybody.

"When someone you're friends with dies so young, it's a kick in the gut. We all think we're invincible at that age."

FIVE

PLAYERS WHO DIED IN THE SERVICE OF THEIR COUNTRY

I t's a different world now. There is no draft and no draft lottery. Most of us learn of the fate of our soldiers through stories that appear on the evening news and daily newspapers detailing conflicts that are often half-a-world away. In times past, every conflict meant something because every male was available for the military once he came of age. Again, it is a different world now.

World War I, World War II, Korea, Vietnam, Iraq, Afghanistan . . . the list goes on and American soldiers continue to serve and American soldiers continue to die. Over the years some used fame, wealth, and family connections to avoid military service, or to have safe, stateside duty. Others, regardless of the personal advantages that they might enjoy in life, felt it their solemn obligation to fight for their country.

Professional athletes have not been immune from military service over the years. And when soldiers prepare for war and go to the fields of battle, some will die. A number of active major leaguers died in the service of their country in World War I and World War II. Others gave the ultimate sacrifice a number of years after their playing careers ended. While they are not included in this collection, omitting them is not meant to diminish their service and sacrifice. That would be wrong. It is, rather, simply a way to remain consistent with the idea of remembering players on these pages who died while still active on their fields of dreams.

Some of baseball's biggest names served in the armed services and were even more heroic and successful on the battlefield than they were on the field. Yogi Berra, Dizzy Dean, Larry Doby, Rapid Robert Feller, Gil Hodges, Enos "Country" Slaughter, Warren Spahn, Hoyt Wilhelm, the great Ted Williams, and countless others all enhanced their already impressive reputations with their battlefield experiences.

For years after World War II, players would regularly leave their clubs for two weeks during the season for their military reserve duty.

But other players were not so lucky. Alex Burr and Elmer Gedeon were both killed in airplane crashes in France. Harry O'Neill was killed at Iwo Jima. Larry Chappell died of pneumonia while serving in the U.S. Army Medical Corps. And Ralph Sharman drowned at Camp Sheridan in Alabama.

Like so many other servicemen, these players were patriots who made the supreme sacrifice so that others could live free in the United States of America and have the opportunity to play baseball.

Unfortunately, these brave players never had the chance to continue playing the game they loved.

ALEX BURR

New York Yankees
Outfield

Bats: Right; Throws: Right
Height: 6 ft. 3 in.; Weight: 190 lbs.

Born: November 1, 1893, in Chicago, Ill.
Died: October 12, 1918, in Cazaux, France

1 Season   .000 BA   0 HR   0 RBIs

KILLED IN A FIERY CRASH

When he made his major league debut with the New York Yankees at the tender age of 20, center fielder Alex Burr no doubt hoped that it was the first day of a long major league career. But his first appearance on April 21, 1914, proved to be his last taste of major league baseball. The Yankees outfield of Roy Hartzell, Doc Cook, and Birdie Cree was a tough one for a young rookie to crack, even on a sixth-place ball club.

With the United States at war, many players were called to serve. And in November 1917, Burr found himself fighting for his country in France as a lieutenant in the U.S. Air Service.

On October 12, 1918, Burr was killed in a fiery plane crash in Cazaux, France. Although there was no official version of how the young outfielder was killed, an aviator friend wrote to Burr's family and noted that the plane in which he was flying burst into flames and crashed into a lake. His body was never recovered.

LARRY CHAPPELL

Boston Braves
Outfield

Bats: Left; Throws: Right
Height: 6 ft.;
   Weight: 186 lbs.

Born: February 19, 1890,
   in McClusky, Ill.
Died: November 8, 1918,
   in San Francisco, Calif.

Purchased by the Boston
   Braves from the
   Cleveland Americans
   in May 1916.

Courtesy of the Baseball Hall of Fame.

5 Seasons   .226 BA   0 HR   26 RBIs   9 SB

VICTIM OF THE PANDEMIC FLU

When Larry Chappell joined the Chicago White Sox from the
Milwaukee minor league club in 1913, the ChiSox paid $18,000 for
the young outfielder's services. Much heralded as an outstanding
prospect, there was a school of thought that in the case of Chappell
the young outfielder may have been hurt by too much publicity, which
led to excessive expectations.

In his rookie season, Chappell played in 60 games hitting just .231 with no homers and 15 RBIs. The 1914 campaign saw him garner less playing time, hitting an identical .231 in just 21 games. He also grumbled over a lack of playing time and at one point was suspended for being out of shape.

Chappell appeared in only one game for Chicago in 1915, going hitless in his only at bat. He was sold back to Milwaukee for just $5,000 in late April, where he remained until August. He was then involved in a trade that brought one of baseball's brightest stars to the White Sox, who just four years later would be part of the Black Sox scandal. Chappell was traded to Cleveland along with Ed Klepfer, Braggo Roth, and $31,500 in exchange for Shoeless Joe Jackson.

Following the trade Chappell played in just three games for Cleveland before being purchased by the Boston Braves in May. He played part of the season with the Columbus minor league club and saw duty in 20 games for the Braves, hitting .226. In 1917, he appeared in his final four major league games.

The Influenza Pandemic of 1918–1919 killed more than 20 million people as nearly 20 percent of the world's population was infected. Larry Chappell was one of the victims of this terrible episode. The once-hot prospect died from pneumonia caused by influenza in San Francisco while serving in the U.S. Army Medical Corps during World War I.

ELMER
GEDEON

Washington Senators
Outfield

Bats: Right; Throws: Left
Height: 6 ft. 4 in.;
   Weight: 196 lbs.

Courtesy of the Baseball Hall of Fame.

Born: April 15, 1917,
   in Cleveland, Ohio
Died: April 20, 1944, in St. Pol, France

1 Season   .200 BA   0 HR   1 RBI

WAR HERO KILLED
OVER FRANCE

Any discussion of Elmer Gedeon the professional athlete pales in comparison to Elmer Gedeon, an American soldier. No one will ever know just how successful Gedeon might have been in the major leagues. He was a two-time 120-yard high hurdles and 70-yard high hurdles champion at the University of Michigan. He played end on the football team and was a star first baseman/outfielder on the baseball team. At the age of 22, he signed a contract with the Washington Senators and went off to play America's Pastime.

Initially after signing his professional contract, Gedeon spent time riding the bench with Washington. When it was decided that he didn't have the experience to fill in at first base or get significant playing time in the outfield, he was sent to the Senator's Orlando farm club. After playing in 67 games, Gedeon was recalled to the parent club, getting three hits in 15 at bats for a .200 average.

On September 18, the long, quick strides that made Gedeon a track star, helped the Senators defeat the Detroit Tigers, 4-2, with a diving, sliding catch in center field robbing Charley Gehringer of what could have been extra bases. The following spring of 1940, he was sent to Charlotte where the swift outfielder hit an impressive .271 in 131 games.

"I remember him as a rookie although I didn't get to know him real well," said Mickey Vernon, who had an illustrious playing career in the major leagues from 1939 to 1960. "The club thought a lot of him. He was a big, tall fellow. The one thing I remember the most is that he could run really well."

His path to a long major league career with the Washington Senators seemed assured. But then World War II intervened. The following March, he was inducted into the U.S. Air Force and trained with the 21st Bomb Group at MacDill Field in Tampa, Fla.

Gedeon proved early on that he was capable of dealing with the realities of war and the situations he was placed in. A leader on the playing field, Elmer Gedeon displayed the same characteristics as a member of the armed forces as well.

In August 1942, in a training flight from Raleigh, N.C., the former outfielder was thrown from a burning B-25 bomber in which he was the navigator. Already injured in the crash, Gedeon returned to the wreckage to rescue his fellow crew members. His heroism resulted in First Lt. Elmer Gedeon being awarded the Soldiers' Medal.

Along with the medal, he received a citation that in part said, "After extricating himself, Lieutenant Gedeon, regardless of the fact the he had suffered broken ribs and severe shock, reentered the burning wreckage and removed Corporal John Barrat, a fellow crew member, who had been rendered helpless due to having received a broken back and broken leg in the crash.

"Corp. Barrat would have been burned to death had it not been for the unselfish action of Lieutenant Gedeon, who in addition to his other injuries, received severe burns on his back, right arm and right leg.

"The heroism displayed by Lieutenant Gedeon on this occasion reflects great credit upon himself and the military service."

The following July, he began training as a pilot on the B-26 Martin Marauders in Oklahoma. In February 1944 while a member of the 394th Bombardment Group from Boreham Airfield in England, Gedeon piloted one of 30 planes that formed a sortie to attack a construction site in France.

On what turned out to be the group's unlucky 13th mission, 30 planes forged an attack on construction works at Bois de Esquerdes. The plane was hit by flak and crashed, killing Gedeon and five other crew members.

The copilot, Lt. James Taaffe, was the lone survivor of the crash.

HARRY O'NEILL

Philadelphia Athletics
Catcher

Bats: Right; Throws: Left
Height: 6 ft. 3 in.; Weight: 205 lbs.

Born: May 8, 1917, in Philadelphia, Pa.
Died: March 6, 1945, in Iwo Jima, Marianas Islands

1 Season   .000 BA   0 HR   0 RBIs

DIED AT IWO JIMA

Along with Elmer Gedeon, Harry O'Neill was the other baseball player with major league experience to be killed in action in World War II. Neither player had much big league experience, but by comparison, the five games that Gedeon played in gave him some first-person memories of his short career. But Harry O'Neill played in just one game, as a defensive replacement, during a game in which his A's were being beaten handily by the Detroit Tigers, 16-3, at Tiger Stadium.

Harry O'Neill was born in Philadelphia and attended Darby High School. Following his graduation he attended Gettysburg College, where he excelled in three sports: football, basketball, and, of course, baseball.

Football in that era was a game of two-way players and O'Neill was an outstanding center who could also play on the defensive line. But on more than a couple of occasions, the outcome of a Gettysburg game depended on his toe, as he was also the place kicker, responsible for extra points and field goals.

The tall athlete also played center on the basketball team, where he led the team in scoring for three years and was also a fine defensive player. For years, Gettysburg alums spoke of his buzzer-beating shots that beat Navy and Ursinus.

But baseball was Harry O'Neill's true love, and in June 1939, as he was about to graduate from college, he signed with his hometown team, the Philadelphia Athletics. Relegated to the bench, the young catcher made only one appearance in his big league career, on July 23, 1939, against the Tigers. Much like Moonlight Graham, the mythical figure in the movie, *Field of Dreams*, O'Neill never got to bat.

The following spring he was off to learn more about the professional game playing in the Canadian-American League for Allentown and Harrisburg.

But before his career could progress any further, O'Neill joined the service, and he was killed in action at Iwo Jima.

RALPH SHARMAN

Philadelphia Athletics
Outfield

Bats: Right; Throws: Right
Height: 5 ft. 11 in.; Weight: 176 lbs.

Born: April 11, 1895, in Cleveland, Ohio
Died: May 24, 1918, in Camp Sheridan, Ala.

1 Season	.297 BA	0 HR	2 RBIs	1 SB

DROWNED AT BOOT CAMP

Ralph Sharman was a fine, young prospect in the Philadelphia A's organization. Coming off his first taste of big league action, he looked like a player who might make an impact on the major league level. In limited action with Connie Mack's team in 1917, the 22-year-old hit .297 in 13 games.

Based on his abbreviated big league action, Sharman at least merited a longer look-see with the Athletics. But World War I took him to the U.S. Army. While swimming in the Alabama River, he drowned on May 24, 1918, just seven months after playing his final game with the A's on October 3 of the previous year.

A TRAGIC SEASON IN CLEVELAND

The 1993 season of the Cleveland Indians was a lost season. It was lost long before opening day. While the team continued to strive to be a force to be reckoned with, no matter what they accomplished on the baseball field, it would be forever overshadowed by a tragic afternoon in spring training. Regardless of what happened during the season, a blanket of sadness and mourning would cover the team and organization for the entire year.

In fact, more than a decade after the events that began on the Indians' only off day in spring training on March 22 1993, there remains an eerie remembrance of pitchers Tim Crews and Steve Olin. For, as the team prepared for the start of the season, it was about to lose its best relief pitcher in Olin and a key newly acquired setup man in Crews.

Both pitchers died as the result of a horrendous boating accident that occurred as their families watched. A third pitcher who was being counted on to be a major contributor to the Indians that year, veteran left-hander Bob Ojeda, was also seriously injured in the accident. He was able to return to the club later that season.

TIM CREWS

Los Angeles relief pitchers Tim Crews, left, Jay Howell, center, and Jim Gott, right, enjoy a night on the town prior to Crews's departure for Cleveland.

Courtesy of Jim Gott.

Cleveland Indians
Pitcher

Bats: Right; Throws: Right
Height: 6 ft.; Weight: 192 lbs.

Born: April 3, 1961, in Tampa, Fla.
Died: March 23, 1993, in Orlando, Fla.

> Signed as a free agent by the Cleveland Indians in January 1993.
> 6 Seasons   11 Wins   13 Losses   15 Saves   3.44 ERA

TRAGIC BOATING ACCIDENT
KILLS RELIEVER

The Cleveland Indians were going to be a team to be reckoned with in 1993. Coming off a 76-86 fifth-place finish in 1992, Manager Mike Hargrove's squad was much improved, particularly on the pitching staff. Veteran southpaw Bob Ojeda, who once won 18 games for the New York Mets, signed with the team as a free agent. His teammate with the Dodgers, right-hander Tim Crews also joined the team, no doubt to be a setup man for the Tribe's outstanding closer, Steve Olin, who was coming off a 29 save season, his finest in the major leagues. Ojeda, Crews, and Olin individually and collectively represented the dawn of better times in Cleveland.

While the sky wasn't necessarily the limit for the Indians in 1993, there were certainly high hopes for improvement in the standings. But during a day off in spring training, the sky literally fell on the franchise as both Crews and Olin were killed in a tragic boating accident that also saw Ojeda seriously injured.

Olin and Ojeda and their families joined Crews and his family at his ranch just outside of Orlando. As darkness fell, the three teammates went on a boat ride together. Crews owned an 18-foot open-air bass boat that could motor along at nearly 50 mph. While riding at a high rate of speed, the boat rammed a new dock extending some 250 feet out into the lake. Olin was killed instantly, Crews died a short time later, and Ojeda was hospitalized wondering why he had been spared. An autopsy later revealed that Crews was legally drunk at the time of the accident.

This horrendous ending to the lives of Tim Crews and Steve Olin happened with a shocking suddenness that was almost impossible to accept. Two players were dead while another was seriously injured. The baseball world was shocked. Teammates and friends were in a state of disbelief. March 22, 1993, was as sad a day as major league baseball had ever known.

"It was an incredible shock," said Jim Gott, an outstanding big league relief pitcher with the Toronto Blue Jays, Pittsburgh Pirates, San Francisco Giants, and the Dodgers, where he and Tim Crews became the best of friends. Relief pitchers pass countless hours together in the bullpen waiting for the call to action. "We became friends when we were both pitching with the Dodgers, hanging out in the bullpen together with our buddy, Jay Howell. We got to know each other and each other's families. 'Crewser' was a cowboy. He loved country and western music and cowboy boots. He grew up in Florida and he and his wife Laurie had just finished building their dream house. He was so excited that he'd bring the blueprints to the bullpen and show us. The place looked great and it was on a lake.

"We were sad to see him move to another team when he signed with Cleveland. Right after the accident, Tim was still alive for a short time. It was an incredibly sad time.

"Tommy LaSorda had a team meeting and all of the bullpen guys were crying. The O'Malley family, who owned the Dodgers at the time, chartered a bus for us all to go to the memorial service."

Crews was a second-round draft pick of the Milwaukee Brewers in 1981. His professional career got off to a promising start that summer as the 20-year-old had a 10-4 record with Burlington of the Midwest League. The following season, Crews had an identical 10-4 mark with Stockton of the California League.

He spent the next two seasons alternating between Class A Stockton and AA El Paso, of the Texas League. Starting the 1986 season with El Paso, Crews had a 5-5 record prior to being promoted to AAA Vancouver of the Pacific Coast League. In 10 games in Triple A, he posted a 2-1 record.

That December, the Los Angeles Dodgers acquired Crews and fellow pitcher Tim Leary in exchange for left-handed hitting first baseman, Greg Brock. At the Dodgers farm club in Albuquerque, Crews boasted a 7-2 record with a 3.62 ERA and 12 saves in 42 appearances. The full-time switch to the bullpen agreed with him, and the Dodgers gave Crews his first taste of the major leagues that season. He responded with a 1-1 record in 20 games with a 2.48 ERA.

He split the next season between Albuquerque (1-1, 2.70 ERA) and the Dodgers (4-0, 3.14 ERA in 42 games).

Except for a brief two-game stint in Triple A in 1989, Crews was in the major leagues to stay. He pitched in 44 games for the Dodgers that season, with an 0-1 mark and an impressive 3.21 ERA. He became a workhorse the following year in 1990, appearing in a career high 66 games with a 4-5 record with 5 saves and an outstanding 2.77 ERA.

In addition to his success as a major league pitcher, Tim Crews also earned the respect and friendship of his teammates.

"He was one of the toughest, most loyal players I ever played with," said Jim Gott. "You just knew he would fight for you. On the mound, he wanted to beat you any way he could. He was not over-powering, more of a sinker-slider kind of pitcher. But he was a tough guy who would get you out by playing cat-and-mouse and by knowing the weaknesses of a hitter.

"He was the perfect setup guy. 'Crewser' never dodged an interview after a tough game. He'd be done with it and immediately get ready for the next game. He was always ready, always in the game, and always prepared."

At the age of 30, Tim Crews had another good season in 1991, going 2-3 with 6 saves and a 3.43 ERA. But for the first time in his big league career, he slumped the following season in 1992 with an 0-3 record and an uncharacteristically high ERA of 5.19. After a successful run in Los Angeles, he was granted free agency after the season and signed with Cleveland on January 22, 1993. Two months later, he was dead.

"It's still very sad, even now," said Jim Gott. "You never expect to be anything other than invincible. I can still remember sitting in the bullpen together and hearing Tim just laugh out loud.

STEVE OLIN

Cleveland Indians
Pitcher

Bats: Right; Throws: Right
Height: 6 ft. 3 in.; Weight: 185 lbs.

Born: October 4, 1965, in Portland, Ore.
Died: March 22, 1993, in Little Lake Nellie, Fla.

Drafted in the 16th round of the 1987 amateur draft by the
  Cleveland Indians.
4 Seasons   16 Wins   19 Losses   48 Saves   3.10 ERA

AN UNKIND GROUP OF
COINCIDENCES LEADS
TO CLOSER'S DEATH

Steve Olin was anything but the prototypical relief pitcher who specialized in closing games. If the standard is a flame-throwing hurler in the Goose Gossage–Al Hrobosky mode, this tall right-hander broke the mold. Olin was not a hard thrower who came over the top with his delivery. He succeeded by tricking opposing batters with his sweeping submarine delivery in which he was almost throwing underhand to the plate.

Steve Olin was a pitcher, in the truest sense of the word, as opposed to a thrower, who could rely on power alone to succeed. What made

Olin special was his ability to outthink the batter, using trickery and his unique delivery.

"You wouldn't say that Steve would light up the radar gun," said former teammate Derek Lilliquist, who spent eight seasons in the major leagues pitching for Atlanta, San Diego, Boston, Cincinnati, and Cleveland. "He was a pitcher with tremendous makeup who was a very fierce competitor. Steve was a submarine-type pitcher, a lot like Gene Garber, who had an uncanny ability to record the last out of the game. It takes a different breed to do that. It comes down to makeup, an extra gene. And he had that."

But it was Olin along with teammates Tim Crews and Bob Ojeda who saw their careers and lives dramatically altered by a deadly combination of coincidences that led to the tragic deaths of Olin and Crews, as well as the serious injuries sustained by Ojeda.

Fresh off of his breakout season in which he firmly established himself as one of the top closers in the game with 29 saves and an 8-5 record in 1992, Olin and his family joined the Ojedas at the Crews ranch in Little Lake Nellie, Fla. Crews and Ojeda were new members of the Indians, both signed as free agents from the Los Angeles Dodgers. Spring training 1993 marked the first time in 45 years the Indians were not preparing for the upcoming season in Tucson, Ariz. But the plan to train in Homestead, Fla., had to be changed due to the damage caused by Hurricane Andrew. So the organization held its spring training camp in Winter Haven, not far from the Tim Crews ranch.

March 22 was the only off day the Indians were to have that spring. A fun day turned to tragedy when the three Cleveland pitchers went for a boat ride on Crews' fishing boat. They rammed into a newly built dock at high speed. Olin, 27, was dead at the scene. Crews was airlifted to the hospital but died early the next morning from lung and head injuries. Ojeda was the only person to survive the crash.

"It was really tough," said Derek Lilliquist. "Mike Hargrove was in his first year as manager of the Indians and he was really big on making us all feel like family. That day was a day off and I remember that I was scheduled to pitch the next day in Port St. Lucie against the Mets. We were supposed to go to that cookout, but my wife suggested that we spend the day at home instead. So I could have been right there with them.

"That night at around 2 A.M., my mother called me. She couldn't believe that I wasn't on the boat with them."

Hopes were high at Indians camp that spring, and Olin, Ojeda, and Crews were three of the major reasons why. A former 18-game winner, southpaw Ojeda was a dependable major league starter. Right-handed setup man Crews would be the perfect transition to Olin and his end game mastery.

In just four years in the major league, Steve Olin was already third on the all-time Indians save list. His 48 saves placed him third on the list behind only Doug Jones (128 saves) and Ray Narleski (53 saves). The sky seemed the limit for this overachiever with the whacky delivery. And yet he remained the same focused, centered person.

"He was a very solid individual," said Lilliquist. "He was very stable and the epitome of a great father. Steve was a true professional and a great person to be around. He liked to have fun, too. I remember one time he and his buddy Kevin Wickander got together and tried to see how many pieces of gum they could chew. Their cheeks were bulging out and they were both drooling, but they both had about 50 pieces of gum in their mouths."

Everything about Steve Olin's career spoke to his possessing the intangibles that don't show up in the box score. Drafted in the 16th round of the 1987 amateur draft, the 410th player chosen was not necessarily expected to make it to the major leagues. But the relief specialist showed early on that he would be the type of ballplayer who would confound the experts. At his first professional stop with Burlington of the Midwest league, the 21-year-old was 4-4 with a 2.35 ERA and 7 saves in 26 games.

He split the 1988 campaign between Kingston of the Carolina League and Waterloo of the Midwest League with a combined 8-2 record with 23 saves. His 1.37 ERA with Waterloo was particularly impressive.

Olin's fast track to the big leagues continued in 1989 where he went 4-1 with Colorado Springs of the Pacific Coast League with 24 saves. That earned him a promotion to the big club in Cleveland where he had a 1-4 record with a 3.75 ERA and one save in his first 25 big league games. While his submarine delivery was especially troublesome to right-handed batters, it was not nearly as challenging for lefties.

Olin once again split the season between Triple A and the Indians in 1990. At Colorado Springs he enjoyed a .301 record and 2 saves in 14 games with an unheard of ERA of 0.66. Upon his return to Cleveland, he fared much better going 4-4 in 50 games.

In 1991, Steve Olin took advantage of his first real opportunity to close in the major leagues. With just 2 saves in his first 75 big league games, he saved 17 games for Cleveland along with a 3-6 record with a 3.36 ERA. That opened the flood gates and set him up for an outstanding 1992 season.

He appeared in a career high 72 games going 8-5 with a 2.34 ERA and 29 saves for the Tribe that year. It was Olin's development as a closer as well as the additions of veteran pitchers Ojeda and Crews that had the Indians' faithful looking for a bright future.

But a hurricane, the club's decision to move its training facilities to the Grapefruit League, and a tragic boat ride forever altered three families and the Cleveland Indians franchise, which had to carry on with its games in spite of the untimely deaths of two players and serious injury to another.

"We had to pull through it," said Lilliquist. "In a sense, we used it to motivate ourselves. As a professional, Steve would have wanted us to move forward. It was a really tough year. But I'm sure he was up there smiling at us the whole time. He was just a class act."

CLIFF YOUNG

Cleveland Indians
Pitcher

Bats: Left; Throws: Left
Height: 6 ft. 4 in.; Weight: 200 lbs.

Born: August 2, 1964, in Willis, Tex.
Died: November 4, 1993, in Montgomery County, Tex.

Signed as a free agent with Cleveland Indians on January 5, 1993.

3 Seasons	3 Wins	3 Losses	1 Save	4.25 ERA

ANOTHER INDIANS PITCHER KILLED IN CRASH

The ultimate year of tragedy for the Cleveland Indians was 1993. Winning and losing seasons come and go, and occasionally every franchise has the thrill of a postseason series. But the horrendous happenings of 1993 will forever be etched in the history of the Cleveland franchise.

The team only had one day off in spring training. On that lone off day, a boating accident took the lives of closer Steve Olin and newly signed setup man, Tim Crews. Another free agent signee, veteran starter Bob Ojeda survived the crash but was seriously injured, although he did return to pitch after that season.

Following the season on November 4, left-handed pitcher Cliff Young was killed in a one-car accident in Montgomery County, Texas. The 29-year-old had gone 3-3 for the Tribe with a 4.62 ERA in 21 games.

"He was a lefty with real good stuff," said his former teammate, another left-handed reliever with good stuff, Derek Lilliquist. "He didn't pitch a whole lot for us because he got hurt a few times. Cliff was a class individual who put himself in the position to be a big league player. It's just a shame that he didn't get the chance to pitch all that much. His accident happened during the off-season."

After the conclusion of the 1993 season, Young was driving on a winding road about an hour north of Houston with his friend John Wilkerson, on their way to pick up a relative from a dance class. At about 9:30 P.M., Young's truck went off of the road and hit a tree. The truck then flipped over, and Young, who was not wearing a seat belt, was thrown halfway through the sunroof and was dead at the scene of the crash.

His friend Wilkerson was wearing his seat belt and received minor injuries.

At the time of the accident, Young's attention was distracted from his driving as he attempted to light a cigarette.

Cliff Young broke into the major leagues in 1990 with the California Angles going 1-1 with a 3.52 ERA in 17 games. He threw a total of 30 innings and exhibited good control for a young left-hander, issuing just seven free passes, while striking out 19. The 1991 season saw Young make 11 more big league appearances with the Angels. He had a 1-0 record in 12 innings with a 4.26 ERA. After a year in the minor leagues he was granted free agency and signed with the Indians.

Just two weeks before his death, Young was granted free agency.

Was the 1993 Cleveland Indians team cursed, or was it simply a case of tragic coincidences?

"It was really tough," said Lilliquist. "I wouldn't say that we were cursed. But we were really tested as professional athletes and as people. Being around people and developing friendships and good relationships is great until they are snatched away. It makes you realize that you can't take anything for granted."

SEVEN

VICTIMS OF MURDER

Violent crime is nothing new to our society. A simple look through a newspaper, or a few minutes watching the local news broadcast, offers numerous examples of murder. Social, economic, and other issues often enter into the reasons for such behavior, but the fact of the matter is that for an enormous majority of our population, murder is the most abhorrent crime imaginable.

Crime statistics come and go and the numbers of violent crimes rise and fall. For instance, in 2003, violent crime across America fell by three percentage points compared with the previous year. But according to FBI statistics, the number of murders across the country that year increased slightly. In 2002, 16,229 murders occurred. The following year, 16,503 people were killed in such a manner, an increase of 1.7 percent.

One of the categories of murders includes motor vehicle theft, most usually victims whose automobiles were carjacked and were killed in the process. Nationally, 30 people lost their lives in this manner in 2003.

One of the things about statistics is that they are nothing more than raw numbers. They don't mean much or hit home until there is a face and a name attached. One of the 30 people killed in 2003 in a motor vehicle theft was a promising first baseman/outfielder with the Cincinnati Reds, Dernell Stenson.

A veteran minor league player, he finally got his chance in the major leagues and was playing winter ball in Arizona to help hone his skills and solidify his spot on the Reds roster. But after a random, gangland-style execution at the hands of the worst that humanity has to offer, Dernell Stenson's major league dream died right along with him on a Chandler, Ariz., street.

Another outfielder was murdered 25 years before Stenson. Lyman Bostock was an outstanding outfielder with the California Angels, with whom he had signed a free-agent contract. After an agonizingly slow start, Bostock hit his stride in mid-season and appeared to be well on his way to a long and successful major league career. But tragedy struck when he was shot to death in a tragic case of mistaken identity. As troubling as his violent death was, the fact that his murderer was a free man walking the streets again a mere 21 months later infuriated many.

Big Ed Morris was a talented, but occasionally hot-headed, pitcher with the Boston Red Sox. He was plagued by control problems that often limited his effectiveness on the pitcher's mound. But as he celebrated at a party held in his honor just before he left for spring training, his life came to a violent end.

Murders are an unfortunate part of our culture. Most similar crimes occur to those who live their lives out of the spotlight. But there are also examples of major league ballplayers who were also killed at the hands of others.

LYMAN BOSTOCK

California Angels
Outfield

Bats: Left; Throws: Right
Height: 6 ft. 1 in.; Weight: 180 lbs.

Born: November 22, 1950, in Birmingham, Ala.
Died: September 23, 1978, in Gary, Ind.

Signed as a free agent with the California Angels on
   November 21, 1977.
4 Seasons   .311 BA   23 HR   250 RBIs   45 SB

SHOT TO DEATH IN A CASE
OF MISTAKEN IDENTITY

Lyman Bostock Sr. never played major league baseball. But he did play in the Negro Leagues from 1938 to 1949 with the Brooklyn Royal Giants and the Birmingham Black Barons. While he never lived his dream of playing against the best of all races, he did see his son, Lyman Bostock Jr., play major league baseball. Unfortunately, a tragic case of mistaken identity limited the younger Bostock's major league career to four seasons and ended his life at the age of 27.

Growing up in Birmingham, Lyman Bostock Jr. went on to play college baseball at California State University before being picked in the 26th round of the amateur draft by the Minnesota Twins in 1972.

A quick two-year stint in the minor leagues was all Bostock needed to make the jump to the big leagues.

The speedy outfielder hit a solid .282 with 29 RBIs in 98 games. That audition prepared him for his first full season with the Twins in 1976, and the 25-year-old paid huge dividends by hitting .323 with four home runs and 60 RBIs. His fine play continued the following season when he hit for career highs in average .336, games played with 153, at bats with 593, runs batted in with 90, and stolen bases with 16. It was a breakout season for Lyman Bostock, giving the impression that he had a long career ahead of him in which the sky was the limit.

Following this great season, in 1977, in which he finished second in the league in batting, he became a big money free agent signing a rich contract with the California Angels. After a horrible start in which Bostock gave part of his salary to charity, he hung in there and got his average up to .296 with 71 RBIs. After a rough start, he had hit his stride and Angel fans were seeing the best he had to offer.

The Chicago White Sox defeated Bostock and the Angels, 5-4, on September 23, 1978. Bostock went two-for-four in his final game. As was normally the case whenever his team visited the Windy City, Bostock stayed with his uncle, Thomas Turner, who lived in Gary, Ind.

Following a dinner with family and friends, Bostock was sitting in the back seat of his uncle's car as it stopped at a red light. A man identified as Leonard Smith pulled up alongside of Turner's car, stepped out of his car, and fired a single shotgun blast into the back seat of Turner's car. Smith was trying to shoot his estranged wife, Barbara, who was Thomas Turner's goddaughter. But he shot Lyman Bostock in the face.

The young man with such a bright future died two hours later at an Indiana hospital.

Leonard Smith was tried for murder and found not guilty by reason of insanity. Smith was incarcerated during his trial, and held for psychiatric treatment afterward. He was then classified as no longer mentally ill and released from Logansport State Hospital just 21 months after he shot and killed Lyman Bostock.

BIG ED MORRIS

Boston Red Sox
Pitcher

Bats: Right; Throws: Right
Height: 6 ft. 2 in.;
    Weight: 185 lbs.

Born: December 7, 1899, in Foshee, Ala.
Died: March 3, 1932, in Century, Fla.

5 Seasons   42 Wins   45 Losses   6 Saves   4.19 ERA

Courtesy of the Boston Red Sox.

KILLED AT A PARTY
HELD IN HIS HONOR

Trouble always seemed to follow Big Ed Morris. A hard-throwing right-hander who spent parts of five seasons in the major leagues, he was plagued by control problems. In more than 600 big league innings, he fanned 256 batters. But he issued free passes to 293. That helped account for his mediocre 4.19 career ERA.

Just how good Big Ed could have been will never be known. Before his death too young at the age of 31, he suffered an injury to his pitching arm during an altercation in a St. Louis hotel elevator. Yet, he had talent and kept coming back.

Big Ed got his start in professional baseball in 1920 pitching with Bradenton, of the Florida State League. The following year, 1921, saw him pitch with Chattanooga of the Southern League, a team he stayed with through most of the 1922 season. Having an outstanding minor league season, Morris was given a brief major league trial with the Chicago Cubs.

The big right-hander appeared in just five games, mostly as a mop-up man. Partially due to his inability to throw strikes consistently, he had an expansive 8.25 ERA in 12 innings. But he was just 22 and would undoubtedly have more opportunities at the major league level based on his live arm.

Morris returned to the minor leagues to hone his craft and gain the necessary experience he would need to crack a major league pitching staff. He spent the next number of years with Chattanooga and Nashville, where he stayed until 1927, when he was traded to Mobile. Following that outstanding minor league season, Morris was sold to the Boston Red Sox.

In 1928, Morris reappeared in the major leagues again at the age of 28 with the Red Sox. He went 19-15, his career best, with a 3.53 ERA in 257 innings pitched. It was also the only season in which he struck out more batters than he walked.

The following season he was 14-14 for the Bosox in 208 innings. Used primarily as a starter, he completed 17 games and threw two shutouts.

The 1930 and '31 campaigns were not particularly good seasons for Big Ed, who had a combined 9-16 record during that time with ERAs over 4.00. The aforementioned arm problems slowed his progress and limited his effectiveness.

Yet, in spite of his unimpressive statistics in 1930 and 1931, he was talented and experienced enough to garner interest from other teams. It was reported that Red Sox owner Bob Quinn had an offer from the New York Yankees for $100,000 for the right-hander. But the trade never had the chance to be consummated.

On the night before he was to leave for the start of spring training in 1932 in Savannah, Ga., Morris was at a party held in his honor in Century, Fla. Six men, including Morris, went to a fishing and hunting cabin on the Escambia River. At one point, Morris argued with Ed Nolan, who was part of the group. Joe White, a gas station operator acted as peacemaker in the exchange. But later, while sitting at a campfire, Morris attacked White for no apparent reason.

The unarmed pitcher pummeled White with his fists. White was knocked to the ground at which time Morris began to kick him. White grabbed a knife and, reaching upward, stabbed Big Ed twice, barely missing the pitcher's heart.

After being taken to the hospital, doctors felt that Morris had a good chance to survive his wounds stating that he had an even chance to recover. But his condition quickly took a turn for the worse and doctors resorted to giving him oxygen in an effort to prolong his life. But on March 3, Big Ed Morris passed away, leaving a wife and two children, as well as unanswered questions as to how he would have fared as a member of the New York Yankees.

Joe White was charged with first-degree murder, but nearly three months after the fatal stabbing was found guilty of first-degree manslaughter in the death of Ed Morris. Joe White was sentenced to three years in prison.

DERNELL STENSON

Courtesy of the Cincinnati Reds.

Cincinnati Reds
First Base/Outfield

Bats: Left; Throws: Left
Height: 6 ft. 1 in.; Weight: 230 lbs.

Born: June 17, 1978, in Lagrange, Ga.
Died: November 5, 2003, in Chandler, Ariz.

Selected by the Cincinnati Reds off waivers from the
    Boston Red Sox on Feb. 23, 2003.
1 Season   .247 BA   3 HR   13 RBIs

YOUNG PROSPECT SUFFERED
GANGLAND-STYLE MURDER

The tragic, gangland-style murder of Cincinnati Reds outfielder/first baseman Dernell Stenson remains one of the saddest and strangest cases in memory. He was found dead on a residential street in Chandler, Ariz., on Wednesday, November 5, 2003. Police regarded the crime as a robbery, suspecting that Stenson's 2002 Isuzu Rodeo was spotted outside a Scottsdale nightclub by the killers. According to reports, Reginald Riddle and David Griffith kidnapped Stenson and drove to Chandler in his car.

With his hands bound by plastic handcuffs and his feet tied together with shoelaces, Stenson apparently put up a fight and was shot several times. He was also run over with his vehicle as he got tangled in his seat belt while trying to escape and was dragged for more than 1,000 feet.

But the case took a strange, more complicated turn when it was learned that just two weeks prior to his death, Stenson had contacted Scottsdale Police over death threats he was receiving from his ex-girlfriend in Indianapolis. The two men arrested and about to stand trial for Stenson's murder were questioned by law enforcement officials, who seized $11,182 from the pair before releasing them. Authorities said that the two suspects were traveling from Indiana, where the jilted girlfriend lived, to Arizona, where Stenson lived.

Another man questioned in the case is in the federal witness protection program. He was arrested for hindering prosecution and renting a hotel room for the suspects after the murder.

The life of Dernell Stenson was violently snuffed out just when it appeared that all of the dedication and hard work the muscular young man so willingly exhibited was just about to pay off.

"He had gotten a chance to play with the Reds and was just starting to find himself," said Rick Burleson, a coach and manager in the Cincinnati system who was also Stenson's manager in the Arizona Fall League. "I saw this guy, because he did not have a tremendous amount of speed, as a fourth outfielder on a major league team, a back-up first baseman, or a power hitter off the bench. He could also be a good designated hitter, in the American League.

"The ball, at times, just rocketed off his bat. He was a strong guy who would have had several years in the big leagues because of his bat. I had Dernell for a few weeks in Arizona and he was a very quiet young man who was extremely polite. I never heard a four-letter word come out of his mouth. He was just a quiet, polite guy who obviously had an outstanding upbringing."

The strange circumstances surrounding his untimely death are a tragic afterthought to a bright young career that was finally reaching its potential. Dernell Stenson was drafted by the Boston Red Sox in the 3rd round of the amateur draft in 1996. He hit just .216 in 32 games with the Red Sox in the GCL League that year. But the strong left-handed hitter had an impressive 1997 while playing for Michigan of the Midwest League, hitting .291 with 15 homers and 80 RBIs in 131 games.

In 1998, he was promoted to Double A Trenton of the Eastern League where he hit .257 with 24 home runs and 71 RBIs. The following season, Stenson began what would be a four-year tenure with the AAA Pawtucket Red Sox of the International League. Playing in the friendly confines of McCoy Stadium, Stenson hit an impressive .270 for the '99 PawSox, belting 18 home runs while driving in 82.

The following season he hit .268 with 23 homers and 71 RBIs, but did not get a late-season call-up in Boston.

In 2001, Stenson slumped to a .237 average with 16 homers and 69 RBIs and the following season hit .250 in Pawtucket with 9 home runs and just 36 RBIs. Upon his promotion to Pawtucket, Stenson put up outstanding numbers but never got a call from the parent club to at least get a taste of major league life. That seeming dead end with the Red Sox organization may have had a negative effect on his production.

Following the 2002 campaign, he was acquired by the Reds off waivers from Boston. Perhaps a fresh start in a new organization could help the big slugger restart his path to the major leagues.

"Sometimes it seems that you've gone as far as you can go in an organization," said Burleson. "The fresh start with the Reds organization for him was big. When he got called up to the Reds at the end of the '03 season, he did some things that opened eyes in the organization."

His power returned in 2003 as he hit 14 homers with 76 RBIs while playing for Double A Chattanooga of the Southern League. In 17 games with Louisville of the International League, Stenson hit 5 round trippers in just 17 games. Finally, on August 13 of that year, Stenson's eight-year minor league sojourn resulted in his call-up to the Reds. In his first big league start, he ripped two doubles and a single against the Houston Astros.

In 37 games with Cincinnati, Stenson hit .247 with three home runs and 13 RBIs in his first taste of major league pitching. In the last series of the season against Montreal, he made three outstanding catches in left field and also homered on the final day of the season.

At the time of his death, Stenson was playing in the Arizona Fall League, preparing for spring training and trying to fine tune his skills to ensure a spot on the Reds major league roster. After a long tenure in the minors, Dernell Stenson had served notice that he was going to be a force to be reckoned with.

While playing for the Scottsdale Scorpions, he hit .394 in 18 games. That average was third best in the league and, as was always his custom, in addition to winning friends and fans on the field, he was also a very popular player on his team and in the league.

Then he was killed in a senseless act of violence.

"I was the manager of that team and everyone on the team was devastated by his death," said Rick Burleson. "He had many friends on the team, but also from other organizations too. Not just the Reds organization. They say that good people often die young. Why that happens nobody knows. It's just a shame. I gave the team the option of stopping the season and going home, or staying. They all wanted to finish the season in his honor.

"There were a couple of different scenarios about what happened. The bottom line is that it was just a random carjacking and murder."

Dernell Stenson touched many lives during his relatively short baseball career. An act of greed and violence cost a fine young man his life. And it seems obvious that he also had an immediate future in the major leagues.

"Whenever I think of him I think of a late-blooming outfielder who would have had an impact in the major leagues," said Rick Burleson. "He came to play."

Reginald Riddle and David Griffith were charged with numerous crimes, including first-degree murder, kidnapping, and armed robbery. Psychological examinations of Riddle have caused the prosecutors office to reconsider seeking the death penalty for him. In January 2006, Riddle accepted a plea agreement to first-degree murder in the killing. By doing so, he avoided the death penalty. It was then up to the judge, Robert Gottsfield, to decide if the 21-year-old Riddle would be eligible for parole after serving 25 years of his life sentence.

Griffith was scheduled for trial later in the year.

Kevin Riddle, the half-brother of Reginald Riddle, had possession of Stenson's car and pleaded guilty to charges that included auto theft, attempted hindering prosecution, and received a sentence of eight years in prison.

While the wheels of justice continue to turn in this case, there was clearly no justice for Dernell Stenson or his family and friends.

EIGHT

ACCIDENTAL DEATHS

One of the things that can most accurately prove the fragile nature of life is when we see examples of accidental deaths. Life snuffed out due to something so seemingly innocent that it almost seems more of a bad joke than reality. In our own lives there are examples of those whose lives were ended from nothing more than horrible bad luck.

Many examples come to mind such as one former major league baseball player, Aurelio Rodriguez, who was killed while standing on a sidewalk and run over by a car that jumped the curb. People die from falls off ladders and even stepstools. Others have died falling into an uncovered manhole, been killed by a machine they were operating, or even been run over by a tractor they were driving.

The most recent accidental death to impact the baseball world occurred more than 30 years ago when Houston Astros fire-balling right-hander Don Wilson died of carbon monoxide poisoning along with his five-year-old son. The death was officially ruled accidental, but there remain those who feel it was actually a suicide.

While Wilson's accidental death was the most recent, probably the most mysterious was the last train ride taken by future Hall of Fame member Ed Delahanty, of the Washington Senators. Apparently despondent over some complicated baseball wheeling and dealing, the popular outfielder was apparently kicked off of a train near Niagara

Falls and died soon after. Did he accidentally fall while attempting to cross the International Bridge on foot? Was he pushed? Or, did he decide to end his life on a lonely, disappointing night? The answers to those questions and more follow.

The only major league player to die after being beaned in the head is Ray Chapman, of the Cleveland Indians. The talented short-stop was known for crowding the right-hand batters box, a fatal mis-take facing hard-throwing, side-arming, right-hander Carl Mays, of the New York Yankees.

One of the most popular players in the history of the Philadelphia Athletics was reserve catcher Doc Powers. He lit up the clubhouse and was a fan favorite. For years, he was the designated catcher for the great pitcher, Eddie Plank. Powers injured himself in the first game ever held at Shibe Park when he crashed into the grandstand chasing a foul pop.

He finished the game, but was dead two weeks later. Did the con-tact with the wall lead to his death? Was it a misshaped belt buckle, or did two cheese sandwiches seal his fate?

Some of the questions about the passing of these players may never be answered. But regardless of the ultimate causes of death, to a degree, the stories that follow include players who never had the chance to say, "Oops."

JOHN CARDEN

New York Giants
Pitcher

Bats: Right; Throws: Right
Height: 6 ft. 5 in.; Weight: 210 lbs.

Born: May 19, 1921, in Killeen, Tex.
Died: February 8, 1949, in Mexia, Tex.

1 Season   0 Wins   0 Losses   22.50 ERA

KILLED IN A HOUSEHOLD ACCIDENT

The name of John "Smoke" Carden is certainly only known to the most serious baseball historian. But he was believed to have great potential and, as his nickname would infer, he possessed a great fastball.

The big right-hander pitched but one game in his major league career, a two-inning stint for the New York Giants in which he gave up seven hits and five earned runs. But the story of John Carden is a story of unfulfilled potential like few others.

Born in Killeen, Texas, Carden attended Texas A&M University where he established himself as one of the best pitchers in the country. His blazing heater helped the Aggies win the Southwest Conference in 1942 and tie for the title in 1943.

As was the case with so many other young men at that time, Carden enlisted, joining the Marines. He pitched for Quantico in 1944 and 1945 where one of his teammates was future Minnesota Twins manager Cal Ermer. In his two seasons with Quantico, Carden sported an 8-4 and 18-7 record, leaving little doubt that he was one of the best pitchers in the service.

Following his discharge from the Marines, he signed a contract with the New York Giants in May 1946. Later that month, he had his lone major league outing with the Giants. Following that game, he was sent to Richmond where he finished the year gaining experience.

Carden then developed arm problems and had elbow surgery, which slowed his career. In 1947 he split the season with two minor league teams as he recuperated from surgery. He went 1-4 with Sioux City and 3-1 with Trenton. But come 1948, John Carden left little doubt that he was right on the doorstep to the major leagues, pitching an overpowering 11-5 for Knoxville. In 1949, he would be pitching for Triple A Minneapolis, making his final pit stop on the trip back to the major leagues.

But before leaving for spring training with his pregnant wife, Ellen, Carden was working with his father-in-law, John Focke, on a power and electrical pole. He accidentally touched a 2,300-volt power line and was electrocuted. Authorities rushed to the scene, but an hour-long attempt to save John Carden's life failed.

His life was over and the great potential he possessed would never reach fruition.

Ray Chapman

Cleveland Indians
Shortstop

Bats: Right; Throws: Right
Height: 5 ft. 10 in.; Weight: 170 lbs.

Born: January 15, 1891, in Beaver Dam, Ky.
Died: August 17, 1920, in New York

9 Seasons   .278 BA   17 HR   364 RBIs

DIED AFTER BEING HIT ON
THE HEAD WITH A PITCH

No matter what Ray Chapman accomplished on the baseball field, or what he might have accomplished had he lived, the fact of the matter is that Ray Chapman is the only player in the history of major league baseball to die as the direct result of an injury during a game. The outstanding shortstop of the Cleveland Indians was very probably a Hall of Fame candidate based on his first nine years in the majors. But an overcast August day in New York marked the end for "Chappie," very possibly the most popular member of the Indians baseball club.

Cleveland was in the midst of a three-team fight for first place with New York and Boston, as they played the Yankees on August 16, 1920. The Yankees starter was Carl Mays, who was opposed by Cleveland's Stan Coveleskie. With the Indians trying to avenge a four-game sweep by the Yanks in a recent series in Cleveland, the visitors enjoyed a 3-0 lead heading into the top of the fifth inning. The hard-throwing, side-wheeling spitball specialist Mays was on the mound for New York as Ray Chapman stepped up to the plate to lead off the inning.

Mays was known as being a mean pitcher who would quite often dust a batter off with inside pitches. Chapman was a scrappy player who crowded the plate in a crouched stance who was often hit by pitches. But as he led off the inning, it was felt that Chapman was possibly expecting Mays to start him off with a breaking ball away. But Mays threw his first pitch high and inside, literally freezing Chapman, who never moved away from the pitch.

He was hit on the left side of his head and the sound of the impact of the baseball resonated throughout Polo Grounds. Of course, in 1920, batting helmets were not used. Blood ran out of his ears, mouth, and nose.

As medical personnel and teammates rushed to his aid, Chapman lay unconscious on the ground. He was, however, revived and tried to walk off of the field into the dugout, but began to collapse and was carried off the field by his Indian teammates.

As he was taken to St. Lawrence Hospital, the game continued with Harry Lunte taking Chapman's place in the Indians lineup. Cleveland and Coveleskie held off a fierce ninth-inning Yankees rally to win the contest, 4-3. But their minds and hearts remained with the popular Chapman.

Before he was taken from the clubhouse to the hospital, Chapman asked the team trainer to give him the diamond ring his wife of a little more than a year, Kathleen, had given to him as a gift. The trainer, who had put the ring away for safe keeping, returned it to the mortally injured player.

X-rays at the hospital showed that Chapman had suffered a depressed fracture of the left side of the skull. His condition grew steadily worse throughout the evening and surgery was performed just after midnight, even though Chapman's wife had not yet arrived in New York. During the hour-long procedure surgeons remove a piece of the player's skull during the operation.

Although the immediate response to the surgery was encouraging, Ray Chapman died at 4:40 A.M. on August 17, 1920.

After throwing the pitch to Chapman, Carl Mays didn't realize that the high-and-tight pitch had hit the pesky player. Rather, he thought the ball hit off of the handle of the bat. In fact, after hitting Chapman, the ball came out toward the pitcher's mound and Mays fielded the ball and threw to first base. Moments later, he realized what had truly happened.

According to an August 18, 1920, story that appeared in the *New York Times*, Mays said, "Chapman was one of the gamest players and one of the hardest men to pitch to in the league. I always dreaded pitching to him because of his crouching position at the bat. It is the most regrettable incident of my baseball career and I would do anything if I could undo what has happened."

Mays was interviewed by the district attorney's office and was cleared of any wrong doing. Because of his reputation as a pitcher who often pitched inside, some players with the Detroit Tigers and Boston Red Sox attempted to have him banned from the game. But in spite of his unpopularity among his peers, it was generally accepted that the pitch that hit and ultimately killed Ray Chapman was an accident.

After Lunte came in to replace Chapman, he hit just .197 that year, his final season in the major leagues. The eventual successor to Ray Chapman was rookie Joe Sewell, who went on to enjoy a 14-year major league career with a lifetime .312 batting average. After replacing Chapman down the stretch of the 1920 season, he hit .329 in 22 games as Cleveland beat out the defending league champion Chicago White Sox for the pennant.

In the best-of-nine World Series, the Indians defeated the Brooklyn Robins five games to two, to earn baseball honors that year. They played the series with black armbands to remember Ray Chapman.

The young shortstop broke into the major leagues in 1912 at the age of 21, hitting .312 for Cleveland in just 31 games. In his first year as a regular in 1913, he hit the ball at a .258 clip with three home runs and 39 RBIs. A speedy ballplayer, Chapman stole 29 bases that year.

The following two seasons saw him continue to make his mark as an outstanding player, hitting .275 and .270. His best season was 1917 where he hit .302. At the time of his death, Chapman was having the best season of his career, hitting .303 in 111 games and boasting an impressive .380 on base percentage.

Ironically, both Carl Mays and Ray Chapman were both natives of Kentucky. Mays won 26 games that season and 27 more in 1921. He became the first man to win 20 games with three different teams when he did the trick for Cincinnati in 1924.

As a result of the tragic death of Ray Chapman, baseball also made some changes to the basic way the game was played. The established tradition of using the same baseball, often for an entire game, ended. Now new balls were used, and dirty or scoffed baseballs were replaced. This made the ball much easier for to batters to see, particularly at twilight.

A new law also made it illegal for a pitcher to doctor the baseball, making pitches such as the spitball, shineball, and greaseball illegal. Since quite a few pitchers relied on those pitchers, the law was grandfathered in so that hurlers who depended on the spitball were allowed to finish their careers still using that pitch. The last pitcher to earn a victory in the major league throwing a legal spitball was the Pittsburgh Pirates Burleigh Grimes, in 1934.

Finally, in spite of the tragic death of Ray Chapman it was 11 seasons before a major league baseball player wore a batting helmet at the plate. On March 7, 1941, Pee Wee Reese and Joe Medwick of the Brooklyn Dodgers wore batting helmets. Ironically, the Dodgers beat Ray Chapman's old team on that historic day, the Cleveland Indians, 15-0.

Ed Delahanty

Washington Senators
Outfield

Bats: Right; Throws: Right
Height: 6 ft. 1 in.; Weight: 170 lbs.

Born: October 30, 1867, in Cleveland, Ohio
Died: July 2, 1903, in Niagara Falls, Ontario, Canada

Signed with the Washington Senators from the Philadelphia
Phillies in 1902. Inducted into the Baseball Hall of Fame
in 1945.

16 Seasons   .346 BA   101 HR   1,464 RBIs   455 SB

BRILLIANT CAREER ENDS
WITH A TRAGIC FALL

For all of the mystery and wonder surrounding the death of Big Ed
Delahanty, there was little if any mystery to his superior ability on a
baseball field. A .346 lifetime hitter, Delahanty led the league in hitting twice, with a .410 average in 1899 and a .376 mark in 1902. He
eclipsed the .400 mark three times in his career, led the league in hits
once with 238 in 1899, and although not a power hitter, led the league
in home runs two times, with 19 in 1893 and 13 in 1896. Not bad
for the dead-ball era.

One of five brothers to play major league baseball, Ed Delahanty
remains the only player to win batting titles in both the National and
American League. But for all of his accomplishments between the

white lines, it is his ultimate end that has defined the myth that is Ed Delahanty.

After spending 13 of his first 14 major league seasons playing for Philadelphia, Big Ed and Nap Lajoie, two enormous stars in the City of Brotherly Love, signed with the Washington Senators of the American League. Though the team played poorly, in his first season with the Senators in 1902, Delahanty led the league in hitting with a .376 average. Frustrated by the club's losing ways, he apparently made a deal with John McGraw to join the New York Giants for the 1903 season.

But a settlement brokered between the leagues kept all players with their old teams. Forced to play with Washington, having occasional gambling problems, and some marital concerns, Delahanty began to drink heavily. Even though he had a solid .333 batting average, his own personal demons began to take control of the slugging star.

The defending batting champion missed a game in Cleveland, his home town, and was suspended by the Senators. On July 2, on his way to join his teammates in New York from Detroit, Delahanty boarded a Michigan Central Railroad train. During the train ride, Big Ed was a constant source of trouble, drinking and threatening other passengers. With five whiskeys under his belt, he approached other passengers with a straight razor. He even pulled a woman from a berth on the train that he mistakenly thought was his.

Finally, Conductor John Cole intervened after numerous encounters with the star outfielder, and ordered him off of the train at Bridgeburg, the final stop on the Canadian side of the Niagara River, just across from Buffalo.

After being ejected from the train, Delahanty followed the tracks to the International Bridge that separated Canada from Buffalo. A bridge guard identified as Sam Kingston spotted Delahanty walking near the center of the span. The 70-year-old guard recognized that the man on the bridge was quite drunk and tried to grab the 35-year-old professional athlete to pull him to safety.

Seconds later, Delahanty fell from the bridge into the river. The drawbridge was open to allow a freighter, the Ossion Bedell, to pass through. Kingston did say that he heard the man cry out for help. Rumors of suicide, or possibly even murder, surrounded the happenings of that evening for decades. In his book titled *Ed Delahanty in the Emerald Age of Baseball*, author and historian Jerrold Casway uncovered the truth concerning the tragic death of Big Ed.

"There is no question that when he fell off of that bridge into the river that it was an accident," said Casway. "He was trying to catch the team train in New York before it left for Cincinnati. He had a plan for this trip, to continue playing baseball. He had his glove and spikes with him on the train. That bridge is still there and you could easily fall off of it, especially if you were intoxicated.

"Delahanty was a great swimmer, but he fell about 15 feet into a dark, fast-moving current. He never had the time to compose himself in the cold water. Plus, a drunk person can lose his bearings and get disoriented when the water reaches the inner ear. As a result, they often swim down, instead of towards the surface.

"Talk about suicide or murder were just rationalizations of people who didn't want to be sued. The mystery of his death has been solved."

As baseball fans across the country learned that Big Ed Delahanty was missing, a number of clues eventually made it clear to investigators that he was on the train bound for New York to join his team and continue his career with the Senators. A full week went by before his mangled body was found near the Maid of the Mist landing by a worker named William LeBland. Delahanty's body was severely damaged with his left leg missing after being caught in the famous sightseeing boat's propeller.

It was a heartbreaking end to what was a spectacular baseball career. In his first season of professional baseball in 1887 with Mansfield of the Ohio State League, Delahanty hit .355. As a 19-year-old the following season, he hit .408 for Wheeling of the Tri State League and was purchased by the Philadelphia Quakers, where he hit .228 in 74 games. He then hit .293 in limited action the following season before playing in Cleveland for the 1890 season in which he hit a solid .296 in 115 games.

It was back to Philadelphia and the Phillies to stay in 1891, and Big Ed hit .243, the last time he was to hit below .300 for the remainder of his career. In 1892, he hit .306 and led the league in triples with 21. Then he smacked the ball at a .368 clip in 1893 leading the league with 19 homers and 146 RBIs. Over the next two seasons, he hit .407 and .404, followed by a .397 1896 campaign in which he led the league with 44 doubles, 13 homers, and 126 RBIs.

"He was a great all-around ballplayer with a strong arm," Casway wrote. "He was a fine outfielder who had good speed. People like John McGraw and Connie Mack, who were around for a while after he died, thought a lot of him. So there must have been something there.

"As a hitter, he may have been the best of all time. He was a finesse hitter with power. He hit for power in a dead ball era and was the dominant player of his time. As a hitter, he had no equal. He was flawed, but he was a great athlete. Ultimately, age and a lack of conditioning eroded his speed."

Year after year, Delahanty continued to be a dominant force in major league baseball. In the mid-1890s, he played in an outfield with two other Hall of Fame members, Billy Hamilton and Sam Thompson. But as the great seasons continued, his off-the-field problems and heavy drinking also continued. While opposing pitchers couldn't stop him, it was becoming more obvious that he couldn't stop himself from the type of behavior that would ultimately lead to his unfortunate end.

"He never had a job," said Casway. "His job was being Ed Delahanty. He was a man-child who died at 36. He gambled, lived the good life and waited for the first advance of next year's salary. But he was never a habitual problem drinker and never a problem ballplayer. He was a good teammate who always had an open hand to a player in need who would always help with charities as well. The ball players liked him, he was very popular.

"The fans loved him. They could see him in the neighborhood and he'd be in the bars buying beers for people. He was a man-about-town who sought publicity and liked to live his life in the limelight."

He led the league in hitting with a .410 average in 1899 and also led the senior circuit with 238 hits, 55 doubles, and 137 RBIs. Two more solid seasons in Philadelphia were not enough to keep Big Ed happy and he signed a contact with the Washington team of the new American League and nearly doubled his salary.

American League pitchers didn't have any more success against Delahanty than their National League counterparts did as he won the AL batting title with a .376 average with a league-leading 43 doubles.

But a failed deal to play for the New York Giants and other personal problems led Ed Delahanty to a drunken binge that resulted in his being kicked off a train near Niagara Falls.

The rest is history.

Ed Delahanty was elected to the Baseball Hall of Fame 42 years after his death in 1945.

JAMES "DOC" MCJAMES

Brooklyn Superbas
Pitcher

Bats: Unknown; Throws: Right
Height: Unknown; Weight: Unknown

Born: August 27, 1874, in Williamsburg County, S.C.
Died: September 23, 1901, in Charleston, S.C.

Assigned to the Brooklyn Superbas by the Baltimore Orioles
   on March 11, 1899.
6 Seasons   79 Wins   80 Losses   3.43 ERA

VICTIM OF A HORSE
AND BUGGY ACCIDENT

There are many things about "Doc" McJames that will forever remain
a mystery. Born James McCutchen James in South Carolina, his
nickname of "Doc" was more than just a moniker he acquired for no
good reason: McJames graduated from the South Carolina Medical
College in Charleston. But along with medicine, a major love of his
life was baseball. In fact, he was the first University of South Carolina
graduate to play major league baseball.

   The good doctor broke into the major leagues for a cup of coffee
with the Washington Senators as a 20-year-old in 1895. He split his
two starts with a 1-1 record and a fine 1.59 ERA. But control problems would plague him for his entire career as it did in his first crack
at The Show as he walked 16 batters in 17 innings.

He took a regular turn for Washington the following season in 1896, sporting a 12-20 record in 37 games with a 4.27 ERA. In 280 innings he yielded 310 hits and 135 free passes while fanning just 103 hitters. McJames had a 15-23 record in 1897, but led the league in strikeouts with 156. But again, he issued 137 walks and 361 hits in 323 innings. Suffice to say that the young hurler was adept at pitching out of trouble.

Following the season the young workhorse was dealt to the Baltimore Orioles along with Gene DeMontreville and Dan McGann in exchange for Jack Doyle, Heinie Reitz, and Doc Amole, who it should be added, was not a medical professional. McJames pitched just one season in Baltimore but had what had to be considered a breakout season, winning 27 games while losing 15. He pitched a career high 374 innings, gave up just 327 hits and a respectable 113 walks with a 2.26 ERA.

While his baseball career was on the rise, his interest in medicine was just as important. After being sent to the Brooklyn Superbas prior to the 1899 season, he had a respectable 19-15 campaign with a 3.50 ERA. One of the highlights of his season occurred on September 9 of that year when he had a no-hitter going against Boston with two outs in the ninth inning when Hugh Duffy singled to break up his masterpiece. He did, however, win the game, 4-0, for his lone shutout of the year.

McJames then sat out the 1900 season to practice medicine in Cheraw, S.C. But the baseball bug continued to bite and he rejoined the Superbas for the 1901 season, struggling to regain his form as his 5-6 record with a 4.75 ERA indicates.

Although struggling, in August of that year there were rumors spreading in newspapers that Brooklyn was willing to send him to the Chicago Orphans in exchange for Rube Waddell.

Was he destined to continue his baseball career or dedicate the rest of his life to medicine? Sadly, that is a question that will never be answered as the talented young man was injured in a one-vehicle horse-and-buggy accident in Charleston. He was thrown from a carriage by a runaway horse, suffering internal injuries and a fractured arm, and died a few days later after the accident.

MIKE "DOC" POWERS

Courtesy of Joe Dittmar.

Philadelphia Athletics
Catcher

Bats: Right; Throws: Right
Height: Unknown;
  Weight: Unknown

Born: September 22, 1870,
  in Pittsfield, Mass.
Died: April 26, 1909,
  in Philadelphia, Pa.

Purchased from the New
  York Highlanders by the
  Philadelphia Athletics on August 7, 1905.
11 Seasons   .216 BA   4 HR   199 RBIs

MYSTERY STILL SURROUNDS
POPULAR BACKSTOP'S DEMISE

In the 1970s and '80s, Philadelphia Phillies ace pitcher Steve Carlton had his own personal catcher in Tim McCarver. The two played together in St. Louis and developed a comfort zone on the field and a close friendship off the field.

That same type of relationship also existed in Philadelphia many years before, but not with the Phillies. It was on Connie Mack's

Athletics that ace pitcher Eddie Plank and backstop Mike "Doc" Powers became a dynamic duo. Although he had a career average of just .216, "Doc" Powers was a solid receiver who called a fine game, had a good arm, and had a quick release that enabled him to nab potential base stealers. In addition, he and Plank, who won 326 big league games and is a member of the Baseball Hall of Fame, were on the same wavelength when Plank was on the mound and Powers was behind the plate. But their friendship did not end there. In addition to being teammates and the best of friends, Powers, a practicing physician, was also Plank's personal doctor.

Basically, from the time Eddie Plank arrived in Philadelphia in 1901, his regular catcher was pretty much always "Doc" Powers. And while he wasn't much of a hitter, Powers was a veteran presence on the field and in the locker room that his teammates appreciated.

"He was rather quiet, but very intelligent and highly respected," said Joe Dittmar, co-chairman of the Connie Mack Chapter of SABR and also vice chairman of the records committee. "He was a very good defensive catcher who couldn't hit a lick. Doc Powers caught the first game in Philadelphia A's franchise history and also caught the first game at Shibe Park. Of course, that turned out to be his final game."

There was a celebratory mood on April 12, 1909, when the Athletics hosted Boston in what was the inaugural game at Shibe Park, at 21st Street and Lehigh Avenue, in Philadelphia. The enthusiastic crowd of 31,160 fans saw their A's handily defeat Boston, 8-1, behind their ace, Eddie Plank.

But something occurred during the seventh inning of that game that would have a profound effect on the A's organization and the city of Philadelphia. Something occurred that has resulted in a mystery that is still up for debate even today. Catcher Powers went after a foul pop-up, behind home plate. Possibly because it was the first game at the new stadium and he was not familiar with just how much room he had to work with behind home plate, Powers crashed into a grandstand wall going after the pop-up.

The gritty veteran was hurt, but remained in the game, helping his pal Plank earn his first victory of the year. Powers even added a single in four at bats. But following the game, he complained of intestinal pains. His condition grew worse and he underwent the first of three surgeries the very next day.

The popular catcher fought for his life, but succumbed to his injuries on April 28, 1909, at the age of 38. He was thought to have been the first player to die of injuries received on the playing field. But upon further review, there is some doubt as to whether or not the injuries he received crashing into the grandstand wall were severe enough to have killed him.

Newspapers of the day stated that Powers had passed away due to gangrene poisoning in his intestines. The death certificate indicated that the cause of death was acute cardiac dilatation. If all of the infected tissue was not removed in the operations that Powers endured, the infection could well have spread from his intestines and bowel area up to his heart, causing acute cardiac dilatation.

Another account mentioned that he ate several cheese sandwiches before the game, which could have led to distress multiplied by the collision. A trainer with the A's even went on record as saying he felt the cause of Powers's injury was a heavy belt buckle that players wore in those days. The pressing on the abdomen of the buckle could create damage, particularly when leaning against or hitting a wall while chasing a foul pop.

What killed "Doc" Powers? Was it the impact of the collision behind home plate, a belt buckle, or a severe case of indigestion? The truth of the matter is that since no autopsy was performed on the popular veteran catcher, there is no way to determine exactly what killed "Doc" Powers.

"There were all kinds of theories as to what caused his demise," said Joe Dittmar. "They all seem highly unlikely and improbable. I spoke with a number of doctors who agree that the severity of his situation could not have been brought on from banging into the wall, or eating a cheese sandwich, or a wide belt buckle.

"The truth is that they don't know what killed him. Powers died, but we don't know what caused his death. But all the rumored stories were incorrect."

Regardless of what it was that killed "Doc" Powers, it seems very probable that the injury or illness that led to his passing could have been treated today in a matter that would have not only saved his life but also seen him return to the A's later in the season.

After his untimely passing the true popularity of the veteran catcher came to light. He lived in Philadelphia in the off-season where he practiced medicine. During his years with the A's, he developed a loyal following. It was estimated that 10,000 people viewed his remains, and mounted police had to clear a path for his teammates to carry his body into the church for his funeral.

A Massachusetts native, Powers attended the College of the Holy Cross and the University of Notre Dame and was a medical doctor. When he finally got to The Show in 1898 with the Louisville Cardinals, he hit .273 in 34 games as a 27-year-old rookie. His first full season in the major leagues in 1899 was split between Louisville, where he hit .207 in 49 games, and the Washington Senators, where he hit .263 in 14 games.

He resurfaced in the major leagues with the Athletics in 1901 and had his most productive season offensively. He played in a career high 116 games with a .251 average, one home run, 47 RBIs, and 26 doubles in 431 at bats. After that he was relegated to back-up Eddie Plank duty. He hit .264 in 1902 with two homers (his career single-season high) and 39 RBIs. He hit .227 in 75 games in 1903 and .190 in 75 games in 1904.

The 1905 campaign was a wild one for "Doc" Powers. The 34-year-old began the season with Philadelphia. But after 21 games, he was sold to the New York Highlanders on July 13, where he played in just 11 games. But the injury bug hit the A's and Powers was reacquired on August 7 to replace back-up catcher Red Kleinow and sub for injured first baseman Hal Chase, who had broken his nose in a game against Detroit.

The A's played in the World Series that year and Powers went 1-7 in their losing effort to the New York Giants. In his well-traveled season, Powers hit just .156 in a total of 51 games.

He never hit above .182 in his last three full seasons in the major leagues with a .157 mark in 1906, .182 in 1907, and .180 in 1908. But "Doc" Powers wasn't simply on the team for his offensive skills. He was a popular, respected player who not only helped Eddie Plank during his outstanding career, but was often looked up to and approached for advice by many of the players on the team.

"He was a very charismatic individual," said Joe Dittmar. "He was almost like a father to some of the players."

DON WILSON

Courtesy of the Houston Astros.

Houston Astros
Pitcher

Bats: Right; Throws: Right
Height: 6 ft. 3 in.;
    Weight: 205 lbs.

Born: February 12, 1945, in Monroe, La.
Died: January 5, 1975, in Houston, Tex.

Signed by the Houston Colt .45s as an amateur free agent
    in 1964.
9 Seasons   104 Wins   92 Losses

A BRIGHT AND SHINING STAR

Early in his career, Houston Astros pitcher Don Wilson was con-
fused by some because he shared the same name as Jack Benny's
pudgy announcer. But once you saw the tall, lanky right-handed
pitcher, any doubt as to which Don Wilson he was ended. Don
Wilson was first and foremost a talented, overpowering pitcher who
had the ability to carry the team on his broad shoulders.

Wilson possessed a flashing fastball and exploding breaking stuff.
Even from his first full season in the major leagues in 1967 at the

young age of 22, he clearly had the right stuff any time he walked out to the pitcher's mound.

Signed as an amateur free agent by the Colt .45s in 1964, Wilson made an immediate impact. The 19-year-old went just 1-2 for the Cocoa Colts in the rookie league, but he fanned 35 batters while allowing just 23 hits in his first 28 innings of professional baseball. Hurling for Cocoa of the Florida State League in 1965, he boasted a 10-8 record with a remarkable 1.44 ERA. Surrendering less than a hit per inning and striking out nearly a batter per inning, the young phenom had the Houston brass drooling as he firmly implanted himself as a top prospect in the organization.

"He was home grown talent, an original signee who came out of our farm system," said Tal Smith, president of baseball operations for the Houston Astros, who began his first tenure with the team in 1960. "Don was a superb guy, just a great pitcher. He was one of the most intense competitors you'll ever see and an intimidating pitcher. Very much like a Don Drysdale or Bob Gibson, from the same mold. Home plate was his."

Wilson's swift rise to the top of the club's future plans only intensified in 1966 when he amassed an 18-6 record with a 2.21 ERA while pitching for Amarillo of the Texas League. En route to a stellar minor league season, he fanned 197 batters in 187 innings, yielding just 150 hits. The major leagues seemed a certainty for this Louisiana native as he improved with each level he ascended to in the farm system. Wilson's fine season got him a quick look-see with the parent club at the end of the year. In his first big league game that September, he won his debut, yielding just two earned runs in six innings.

His rookie campaign in 1967 saw Don Wilson take a regular turn in the Astros rotation garnering a rather pedestrian 10-9 record, with a fine 2.79 ERA. But on June 18 of that year, he became the first Houston Astros pitcher and only the second hurler in franchise history to pitch a no-hitter. He held the Atlanta Braves without a hit, and to put some real icing on the no-hit cake, the fireballing righty struck out Hank Aaron for the final out of the game. The only other

Houston pitcher to throw a no-hitter was Colt .45s right-hander Don Nottebart, who did the trick against the Philadelphia Phillies on May 17, 1963.

"He was a competitor," said his teammate and friend Jimmy Wynn, who had a 15-year career in the major leagues, 11 of which were with Houston. "When he toed the rubber he went out to win. You like having a guy like him on the ball club who was a big, strong type of player.

"He threw a fastball between 95 and 97 mph. He also had a great slider and would use the change up as well. He'd use his fastball in and out. Like any other pitcher in the '60s and early '70s, he loved to throw inside and then work the hitter outside."

The following season, in 1968, Wilson had a 13-16 record with an ERA of 3.27. But he became a workhorse on the Astros staff pitching 209 innings, allowing only 187 hits while striking out 175. His growing dominance as a pitcher was once again highlighted when he pitched the second no-hitter of his career on May 1, 1969, against the Cincinnati Reds. What made that jewel of a game even more special was that on the previous night, Reds powerful right-hander Jim Maloney had thrown a no-hitter against the Astros. So these two outstanding pitchers threw back-to-back no-hitters.

"We had gotten off to a horrible start that year and then Jim Maloney no-hit us and our record was something like 4-and-20," said Tal Smith. "Then he came back and pitched a no-hitter for us the very next night. It got us back on track. Don just could not tolerate losing."

On the field, Wilson's teammates got a real appreciation for the powerful right-hander and his determination during that game.

"During that game, Dave Bristol, Pete Rose, and Johnny Bench were all over Don, calling him names and trying to dent his confidence," said Jimmy Wynn. "After he struck out Bench for the last out of the game, he started running toward the Reds bench to try to get at Dave Bristol. Fortunately, Doug Rader got to him first. He was really pissed. Don was such a competitor that the adrenaline was really flowing. It's a good thing Doug got to him because he probably would have been suspended. I was way out in center field and there was nothing I could do right then."

A determined and dominating pitcher during the game, Wilson was a quiet and friendly teammate off the field who led by example. He was always at the ballpark on time and acted like a professional at all times. That's not to say that he didn't have a temper.

"Don was an emotional guy," said Larry Dierker, who won 137 games during his 13 years with Houston, nine of which he and Wilson headed up the rotation. "He was pretty laid back. But if something struck a nerve with him, he could become Superman. He was mostly quiet, kind of like a volcano just looking like a beautiful mountain until it went off. After Jim Maloney pitched that no-hitter against us, Don really got his adrenaline flowing and was just unhittable. He carried the entire team on his back. He had a deep well of strength.

"We were friendly, but not best friends. At the park we had a friendly rivalry that was unspoken, but it was definitely there. We both wanted to be the lead man in the rotation and be the ace of the staff. Some years he was better than me, and others, I had the upper hand. But if one of us went out and pitched a good game, the other wanted to go out and do one better.

"I had a lot of admiration for him."

The young fireballer continued to improve, winning 16, 11, 16, and 15 games from 1969 through 1972. In 1971, he represented the Astros on the All-Star team. After going 11-16 in 1973, he had an 11-13 record in 1974. That season he almost became the second National League pitcher to throw more than two no-hitters. He had no-hit the Cincinnati Reds through eight innings, but in a strange game, trailed on the scoreboard, 2-1. Astros manager Preston Gomes lifted Wilson for a pinch hitter in an effort to at least tie the ballgame. That ploy failed and reliever Mike Cosgrove yielded a hit to Tony Perez in the ninth inning to foil the no-hit bid.

During much of his career with the Astros, Don Wilson pitched for teams that weren't quite good enough to compete for postseason play. That was a part of his career that he and his teammates found very frustrating.

"Losing frustrated him much like it frustrated a lot of us," said Jimmy Wynn. "He pitched on a certain level and he expected to win. Being an expansion team, we were sort of a makeshift team in those days. Many of the players who were on the team were let go by other organizations. But we all wanted to win and Don absolutely pitched his heart out for us."

In September 1974, no one knew at the time that the 29-year-old had pitched his final game in the major leagues. On January 5, 1975, Wilson and his five-year-old son, Alex, were found dead in their home of carbon monoxide poisoning. Wilson was found in the passenger seat of the family car in the garage. His son was found in an upstairs bedroom. Another child, nine-year-old Denise, was critically ill, and his wife, Bernice, had a bruised jaw.

The circumstances surrounding the death of this talented pitcher and his son still are steeped in mystery. According to the Harris County medical examiner, Don Wilson was legally drunk at the time of his death. His alcohol content was .167, while the legal limit in the state of Texas is .10. If he were pulled over driving his car, Wilson would have been booked for driving while intoxicated.

In February 1975, R. Joseph Jachimcyzk, medical examiner, ruled the deaths of Wilson and his son to have been accidental. He felt that the pitcher could have turned the engine of the car on to warm himself late at night in his garage. The pitcher's wife told police she had amnesia of the events leading up to the time in which her husband's body was found. Police said there was no evidence to suspect murder or suicide.

"He was a very personable guy," said Tal Smith. "Everybody on the team loved him, just a good guy to be around. In '74, I was working with the Yankees and we had discussions about trading Mel Stottlemyre for Don.

"I thought very highly of him. I felt very badly when I found out about his death. It was a tragic loss."

The untimely death of such a young man also takes its toll on his teammates, who not only lost a friend on the team, but suddenly realized that they too were not invincible.

"When Don Wilson died, it really shook me up," said Larry Dierker. "He was my age and he lockered right next to me. I was at my parents' house in Los Angeles over the holidays when I heard about it. This was the first time I ever had to accept the death of someone my own age. As we get older, of course, it happens more often. But I was almost in a trance. I couldn't assimilate it or accept it.

"They had an open casket at his funeral and it didn't even look like Don. All that week it felt kind of surreal. Then with time, it sort of fades. But when someone close to you passes, it comes back and you feel it again."

His good friend Jimmy Wynn was shocked by his death.

"We lived about 15 minutes away from each other," he said. "I woke up that Sunday morning and saw on the TV that he had been found dead in his car. I still had my pajamas on, but I jumped in my car and drove over to his house. He was still there, sitting in his car.

"He could have been one of the great right-handers in the game. A guy you would mention in the same breath as Bob Gibson and Juan Marichal and Tom Seaver. Off the field, he was the type of guy who would do anything for anybody. He was just a great guy and a really good friend."

Pallbearers at Don Wilson's funeral included Bob Watson, Dierker, Dave Campbell, Roger Craig, Mike Cosgrove, and Robert Gallagher.

NINE

SUICIDE

I t's hard for many to contemplate how any healthy, successful person could even think of ending his life. Certainly, one person's estimation of success and happiness could be completely different from another's. And for the past number of years, the controversial topic of assisted suicide has become a very public battleground for those with strong views on both sides of the issue. But clearly, the decision to end one's life is a serious and troubling happening. To the typical well-adjusted person, the thought of suicide just does not occur.

While the final statistics vary every year, suicide is often near the 10th leading cause of death in the Unites States. The numbers tell us that men are four times more likely to end their life than women. According to the World Health Organization estimates, worldwide it seems that more than 800,000 people kill themselves annually. In fact, it has been calculated that one person commits suicide every 40 seconds.

Is the risk for suicide inherited? Certainly many illnesses and physical conditions have a tendency to run in families, such as high blood pressure, high cholesterol, heart disease, and diabetes. But not all illnesses involve just physical health. There is evidence that genetic factors can contribute to other health issues that could increase the risk for attempted suicide.

The list includes such maladies as bipolar disease, major depression, schizophrenia, alcoholism, substance abuse, and other personality disorders. While these disorders can be passed on from generation to generation, the increased risk for suicide will also be present.

An added circumstance in the sad story of Willard Hershberger was that his father and uncle took their own lives. Not only did he probably inherit some of the demons that caused two close relatives to end their lives, but he may well have been predisposed to do the same thing.

Had he lived his life in this day of mental health awareness, his family history and fragile state would have probably led to intervention by health care professionals who may have been able to keep him from killing himself. But sadly, that was not the case.

While there have been suspicions about the ultimate end of players such as Len Koenecke and Don Wilson, in the history of America's Game, only one player, Cincinnati Reds receiver Willard Hershberger, definitely took his own life. Hershberger was a fine second-string catcher who played so well when he got the opportunity that he might have become a starter, had he lived. But he was a high-strung individual who was often the brunt of kidding from his teammates. His fragile psyche must have been like a time bomb that started ticking early in his childhood.

His career and life ended in a Boston hotel room.

Courtesy of the Baseball Hall of Fame.

#5

WILLARD HERSHBERGER

Cincinnati Reds
Catcher

Bats: Right; Throws: Right
Height: 5 ft. 10 in.;
   Weight: 167 lbs.

Born: May 28, 1910, in
   Lemoncove, Calif.
Died: August 3, 1940, in Boston, Mass.

Traded to the Cincinnati Reds from the New York Yankees for
   Eddie Miller and $40,000 cash on December 3, 1937.
3 Seasons   .316 BA   0 HR   70 RBIs

A TROUBLED SOUL

The 1940 edition of the Cincinnati Reds were coming off a great season the previous year in which they won the National League pennant, only to lose to the New York Yankees in the World Series. Hope always springs eternal, but the '40 Redlegs seemed to have a realistic chance to get back to the Fall Classic and have things go their way.

   One of the trademarks of a championship caliber club is having the depth to withstand injuries. The Reds had great frontline players like eventual Hall of Fame catcher Ernie Lombardi, first baseman Frank McCormick, and outfielder Mike McCormick. The pitching staff was anchored by ace Bucky Walters, who along with Paul Derringer, Junior Thompson, and Jim Turner, gave the Reds at least a chance to win just about every game in which they pitched.

As is the case with most every major league club in every major league season, at some point of the year, the bench players will be called upon to fill in at key times. Such was the case when regular catcher Lombardi was felled by a series of injuries. That's when highly regarded back-up Bill Hershberger was pressed into duty.

"He was the nicest guy in the world," said Bill Werber, an infielder who hit .277 in Cincinnati that season and is the only living former teammate of Babe Ruth and Lou Gehrig. "Hershie would have been a regular catcher just about anywhere else, but not with Ernie Lombardi there. He sprained his ankle and Hershie was put in to catch.

"Hershie was usually the first person off the bench to pinch hit. He was a helluva fine boy. He didn't drink and loved outdoor sports. He was really excellent with a rifle. They always hated to see him come up to a shooting gallery because he was always going to walk away with some of the prizes."

While playing for the Newark Bears in 1937, Hershberger was voted the outstanding catcher in the International League that season. The Bears went on to win the Little World Series.

After being acquired from the New York Yankees in a trade, Hershberger had been a more than adequate fill-in, hitting .276 in 49 games in 1938. The following season, he had career highs for games with 63, at-bats with 174, and batting average with a lofty .345. He played in three of the World Series games against the Yankees with a .500 batting average.

As Lombardi languished on the injured list, the play of Bill Hershberger was so impressive that rumors spread of a possible trade involving Lombardi. The 30-year-old backstop filled in admirably with a .309 batting average through 48 games. This figured to be his best season, getting more and more playing time to be a more than adequate fill-in for Lombardi. The strong Cincinnati club seemed to have a great chance to repeat as National League champions.

But Bill Hershberger had demons present in his life. Years before, in 1928, his father committed suicide. Then his father's brother also took his own life. Often the brunt of kidding and practical jokes by his teammates, Hershberger probably felt the need to always be at his best on the playing field. Few understood his fragile mental condition or his tragic family history.

"Research has shown that there is a correlation between mental health and genetic disposition," said Jennifer DiStefano M.A. SAC. "If someone in your family has some type of mental illness, not just depression, you have three times the chance of having mental illness. Ninety percent of people who attempt suicide have had a mental illness of some sort."

The likeable Hershberger tried to be one of the guys, but some of the good-natured needling that all ballplayers endure was something he took to heart much more seriously than the typical player.

"He was a hypochondriac and I know the kidding bothered him," said Werber. "But ballplayers are always getting after each other. Some can be really cruel, even if you love the guy. And he was one of the most popular guys on the team."

During a game on July 31 against the New York Giants, the Reds coughed up a 4-1 lead, eventually turning victory into a 5-4 loss. But in spite of a big lead in the standings and the general understanding on the team that the game only represented one game and nothing more, a combination of things caused Bill Hershberger to begin a downward spiral that would ultimately end with his death.

With two outs in the ninth inning, Walters gave up a walk to Burgess Whitaker and then a home run to Mel Ott. The next batter walked and then Harry Dannings hit the game-winning home run for New York.

Blaming himself for calling bad pitches in the final inning, Hershberger fell into a deep depression. Although it was just one game in a long season, he simply could not let the ninth-inning loss go.

Because of the kind of person he was and his psychological makeup, he absolutely felt that he was responsible for the turnaround and loss.

"It was an awfully hot, humid day and Hershie wasn't feeling well," said Werber. "Our manager, Bill McKechnie, gave him a spoonful of brandy to try to pump him up. Bucky Walters was our best pitcher. Then all of a sudden, it happened so quickly, bing, bing, bing, bing. We had lost the game and Hershie blamed himself for that.

"On the train to Boston, he just sat in his berth shaking his head, saying if Lombardi had been in there it never would have happened. He said he was no asset to the ball club. I just said to forget about it because it was just one game. We still had a 9- or 10-game lead in the standings. It was only one game.

"We had an off day the next day in Boston. I had breakfast with Hershie, and to try to get his mind off of it, I asked him if he'd walk with me to the Massachusetts Casualty Building, where I had some business. Then we went to the movies. After that, we walked back to the Copley Plaza Hotel."

While his manager and some teammates tried to lift Hershberger out of his depressed state, there was probably little that anyone could have done. Mental health awareness in 1940 was nothing like we see in the twenty-first century. Depression can be treated now, but there were no mental health professionals to intervene in Willard Hershberger's troubled state.

"If a person who is depressed and has a mental disorder has a situation in their life, it can put them into a tail spin," said Jennifer DiStefano. "They want to get rid of the pain so they look at ways to do so. With a family history of depression like his and with his father and uncle committing suicide, the predictors were very high that the person is a real candidate for hurting himself. His family history was a huge factor."

Even though the Reds left New York and moved on to Boston, Hershberger could not get the blown game against the Giants out of his mind. Regardless of the numerous efforts of his manager and some teammates, including Werber, he continued to focus on the lost game.

Cincinnati and Boston were scheduled to play a double-header on August 3, but Hershie never showed up at the ballpark. He was eventually found dead in the bathroom of his hotel, the Copley Plaza Hotel. The coroner said that his death was caused by an "incised wound of the neck."

"He had taken off all his clothes, spread newspaper in the bath tub and hacked at his throat," said Werber. "He hit his aorta and bled to death. It was a mental thing. His father and uncle had killed themselves also.

"We all felt badly. In fact after we won the World Series that year, we voted a full share of the World Series, $5,860, to his mother. I felt badly about it. We all missed the fellow."

With Lombardi still hobbled with injuries, until he was able to return, the bulk of the catching for the Reds was handled by coach Jimmy Wilson, who was activated for the remainder of the season.

The death of Bill Hershberger shocked his teammates and the rest of the league. He remains the only confirmed case of a major league player to commit suicide during the season.

The Reds went on to win the National League pennant that season with a 100-53 record, getting them to the World Series for the second consecutive year. Just how much Bill Hershberger could have accomplished over the following years will forever remain a mystery. While he evidenced the talent and ability to be a productive major league baseball player, his family history and the demons that were never far from the surface of this troubled person's life spun out of control after the Giants Hank Danning hit that game-winning home run just a few days prior.

In an eerie coincidence, 14 years after Bill Hershberger's unfortunate suicide, the man he was filling in for behind the plate, Ernie Lombardi, also tried to end his life. In 1953, he and his wife were visiting his sister and brother-in-law. Lombardi was suffering from a growing depression, and he slit his throat in the bathroom. Unlike his former teammate, however, Lombardi survived his wound and overcame his depression, passing away of natural causes in 1977.

INDEX OF PLAYERS